Some Things Go Bump in the Night!

30 Famous Haunted Hotels, Inns, B&Bs, and Restaurants

By
Deborah L. Davis

PublishAmerica
Baltimore

First printing

PublishAmerica has allowed this work to remain exactly as the author
intended, verbatim, without editorial input.

Hardcover 978-1-4512-8632-8
Softcover 978-1-4489-4064-6
PUBLISHED BY PUBLISHAMERICA, LLLP
www.publishamerica.com
Baltimore

Printed in the United States of America

Dedications

To my husband, Gary, who has stuck with me for thirty-three years and is the "wind beneath my wings" even with all of his medical problems. He is always there, giving encouragement and praise.

To my son Ben and his wife Casey, for always being there for us and I have no doubt that they always will be. They are the lights in our lives.

To my family...Dad, brothers, their families, and Gary's family. They have been there during our lowest times with help and understanding.

To my Mom, who is no longer with us. She was a great influence in my life and will remain forever in my heart.

And, to God for giving me the strength and courage to go after my dream of writing and the determination and ability to reach it.

Love,
Deb

Author Bio

My name is Deborah L. Davis (Debbie) and I live in a small town in Georgia, close to Chattanooga, Tennessee. My husband, Gary, and I have one son…Ben. We live with our two dogs in a townhouse and love it!

I have been a writer for eight years and I ghost write books for other people as well as doing my own. I always wanted to be a writer and now my dream has come true. Writing is my way of retreating from the problems of everyday life. My husband is very ill and requires attention along with my having Multiple Sclerosis. Some days it's pretty hard to go, which is where my writing comes in.

I used to teach computer programs at a huge photography studio. I also taught grammar and time management. This has prepared me for my work as an author.

Preface

This book is a compilation of thirty haunted hotels, inns, B & Bs, and restaurants. Each has its own chapter along with their contact information and website. There is also history and, of course, the ghost stories.

I have done phone interviews with all of them and even visited some to get the experience of visiting a haunted hotel. The hotels were beautiful with a very welcoming staff and fantastic rooms!

Many people like to read about paranormal experiences, or even plan a trip to a haunted hotel. These stories are tried and true and I'm sure you can pick one out that is close to home. They are scattered throughout the United States.

So...lock your doors, get a cozy comforter, and turn ON the lights. You are about to begin a journey that will make your hair stand on end!

Table of Contents

Glossary of Terminology and Equipment

Credit given to PEER (Paranormal and Environmental Explanations from Research) as well as Steve McNaughton, Chestnut Hall B & B

Audio Recorder: The audio recorder is perhaps one of the simplest pieces of equipment to use on an investigation; yet, it can become one of the most important. Not only does it record interviews with property owners, but it can also record sounds that were not heard during the investigation. Countless EVPs (electronic voice phenomena) have been documented as answers to questions during investigations. Many questions are asked in an attempt to establish who the spirit is and why it's present, so don't dismiss the audio recorder. If you buy an analog recorder, be sure to get one with an external microphone so you can eliminate some of the recorder's internal mechanical noises.

Camcorder: There are several types of video recorders, analog and digital. They use a variety of media tapes and cards or disks and there are other options and accessories to consider. The one accessory that I could not do without however is the additional infrared light, which extends the range of the night vision up to one hundred feet.

Digital Camera: The digital camera is the most commonly used piece of equipment during paranormal investigations. The digital camera does not require the changing, storage, and development of film and can provide quick and immediate verification of an anomaly captured on the disk.

EMF (electromagnetic field): Spirits use energy to make things happen. It might be to move around themselves, make other things move, or even make themselves manifest as an orb, ectoplasm, or as a visible being. It is also speculated that they have some energy of their own, but many times will zap the energy from a nearby source such as a battery, or directly from the atmosphere causing a sudden drop in air temperature. When this energy (known as an electromagnetic field) is concentrated into one location, it can be detected with the appropriate equipment, an EMF detector.

EMF Detector: During investigations, I use two types of EMF detectors. The EMF detector I use to take base readings (the property's normal reading) of an area is the GausMaster. Using a needle gauge and an audio signal, it will quickly let you know if there is an electrical anomaly present. In addition to the GausMaster, a KII EMF detector is recommended. This device uses a series of five lights to indicate the presence of electrical discharges and has been said to be of assistance in having communications with spirits through a series of questions that can be answered with a 'yes' or 'no.'

EVP (electronic voice phenomena): During interviews, vigils, and investigations, I used an audio recorder or a camcorder. Sometimes, when recordings are played back, voices that were not heard during the real time conversation are present. Sometimes these voices are clear and distinguishable while other times they can barely be made out. Sometimes it's not a voice, but a noise such as footsteps, doors opening and closing, tapping, or knocking.

Ghost Hunt: A ghost hunt is performed at a location where there has been no previous evidence of a haunting. This is sometimes a more casual event utilizing less staff and equipment.

Ghost Investigation: A ghost investigation is performed when there have been reports of a haunting that has already taken place. The investigation is approached with a plan of action to answer the what, where, when, who, and how questions.

Infrared: The invisible portion of light that makes it possible to see in the dark. Infrared lighting is what is used by video cameras and camcorders to allow recording in a building in the dark or outside at night when it is impractical to use spot or floodlights.

Intelligent Haunting: The intelligent haunting is just that. One might see a partial or full-bodied apparition. Someone might answer a question or move an object upon request or one just might experience a bump in the night. A person may smell an odor such as smoke when there is none to be found. One may see an orb, a cloud of ectoplasmic mist, but most commonly, a shadow will pass in a person's peripheral vision. These spirits are grounded or earthbound, continuing to exist or live in this plane.

Orb: A circle, a sphere, or a round object related to the energy of a spirit that is often captured on film. In the paranormal field, it is an object captured on film or seen with the naked eye. Many if not most paranormal skeptics do not believe that an orb is related to the energy of a spirit. They believe that all orbs are nothing more than an error or flaw in the camera's ability to properly focus or it is a piece of dust, pollen, or moisture that is floating in the air and too close to the camera lens. Although I will agree that some cameras do have this problem, I do not agree that all orbs captured on film are dust, pollen, or moisture just as I do not believe that everything that falls from the sky is always rain and can be nothing else.

Residual Haunting: This type of haunting can best be thought of as if a person were watching a video or movie. An object or a place can capture the energy of an event and when atmospheric conditions allow, the event will be played back over and over as if recorded in time. Keep in mind that a piece of tape used in audio and video recordings is just film to which the images and sounds can adhere. One cannot interact with residual hauntings; one can only see or hear them as they repeat themselves, trapped in time. How many times have you heard a door close or someone walk up or down the stairs or hallway? That just might be a residual haunting.

Thermal Detector: Like all the other pieces of equipment mentioned in this list, the thermal detector comes in several different styles and has multiple purposes. There are detectors that will read surface temperatures and ones that will read air temperature. The latter is perhaps the most usable and accurate for paranormal investigating since a drop in air temperature can indicate the presence of a spirit.

Vigil: On occasion, investigations lend themselves to a period of time when persons will gather to sit, in an attempt to communicate with spirits that may be in that area. This has nothing to do with a religious ceremony or the use of an Ouija Board. During a vigil, many prefer to take the time to be still and quiet, only to ask questions in hopes of having a communication with a spirit. Tape recorders, thermal scanners, camcorders, and EMF detectors will be used to gather, verify, and validate any anomalies.

Chapter 1
The Grande Colonial

Grande Colonial Hotel La Jolla
910 Prospect Street
La Jolla, CA 92037
Reservations: (888) 530-5766 Local: (858) 454-2181 Fax: (858) 454-5679
Email: info@gclj.com
Contact: Leslie Araiza email: laraiza@gclj.com
Website: http://www.thegrandecolonial.com/

Leslie Araiza was a very gracious hostess. She talked with me about the ghostly happenings at the hotel and took me on a tour. She is a very sweet person and even gave me a big hug when I left. She gave me a complimentary room and I did not have to pay for anything!

When I arrived at The Grand Colonial, La Jolla they were having a torrential rain. As I got out of the cab, we had to walk through rain about three inches deep, just to get to the hotel.

It was beautiful! So warm and toasty with smiling faces ready to greet me. All of the staff was so friendly and ready to meet my every need.

The room was lovely! Mint green with white trim, just the kind of room you would expect in California. The bed was made up to look like it was out of a magazine. I had a huge desk to work on, a big screen television and all of the towels were made up in little decorations

The beach was breathtaking. I had a porch outside of my room and the sounds and smells were so relaxing.

I did not have any paranormal experiences, but I guess ghosts are never there when you need them!

History

The Four Diamond Grande Colonial Hotel, located on popular Prospect Street in the heart of La Jolla, California, is the seaside town's oldest original hotel and on the registry of Historic Hotels of America. The Colonial Apartments and Hotel, as it was known when it opened in 1913, was the talk of the town and a foundation for the community.

The original white, wood-framed Colonial Apartments and Hotel, designed by Richard Requa, was described as, "a perfectly appointed apartment hotel, with the finest sun parlor and lobby overlooking the ocean on the Pacific coast."

George Bane, who became sole owner of the Colonial in 1920, realized the tourist potential of this picturesque seaside town and decided to give the Colonial a whole new look. In 1925, he commissioned architect Frank Stevenson to design a hotel that would "rival anything in the West." It was a huge undertaking. The existing building was moved to the rear of the property and a new, four-story, concrete, mixed-use building was erected in its place. Completed in 1928, the new Colonial Hotel had the first sprinkler system west of the Mississippi; solid, unsupported, reinforced cement stairways and fire doors that still exist in the structure.

Even with its safety features, the Colonial was breathtaking. The "sunburst" design of windows and semi-circle domes of leaded glass above the French doors uniquely captured the sunlight and drew it into the hotel. Inside, the new interior included colonial fireplaces with marble hearths, ornate chandeliers and richly colored sofas and chairs. Rooms were available for $25 to $50 per month. Bane said of the new Colonial, "I've always had confidence in La Jolla, and I still do. This building is the concrete expression of my faith."

After opening the new Colonial, Bane had leased the entire property to a "Hollywood man" named W. S. Beard. Unhappy with the way Beard was running things, Bane reorganized the business in 1931, and R.C. Bugler was brought in as the manager. One year later, a more solid financial plan was drawn for the hotel and the rest of La Jolla grew up around this community cornerstone.

The La Jolla Drugstore, next door to the Colonial, was soon woven into its history. In 1926, the store was purchased by Kansas native Silas O. Putnam, and moved inside the Colonial. Putnam had spent one winter in Southern California's temperate climate and decided to make La Jolla his home. After he bought the drugstore and moved it to its new home, he added an ice cream parlor on the sidewalk that served up chocolate sodas and banana splits.

Later on, the Colonial was a temporary home to some of Hollywood's up and coming stars that were performing at the La Jolla Playhouse, founded by Peck. Charlton Heston, Dorothy McGuire, Groucho Marx, Jane Wyatt, Eve Arden, Pat O'Brien, David Niven and many other celebrities occupied the hotel well into the late 1950s.

During the World War II years, the Colonial became home to many of the "top brass" from nearby Camp Callan. While the men were at Camp during the day, their wives volunteered for the local Red Cross. At night, the hotel's sunroom was partitioned to create accommodations for single servicemen. In 1960, the drugstore needed more space, so Putnam's son, "Putty" moved the establishment to new quarters, much to the chagrin of the community. Over time, the once grand hotel fell into a state of disrepair.

In 1976, three local partners purchased the Colonial for approximately $1 million. The Colonial's name was changed to the Colonial Inn. Over the next four years the hotel underwent a $3 million restoration that brought back its original grandeur. The property was designed "like an elegant, European hotel" by San Diego's Robert Carlisle. No expense was spared—from mahogany trim and wood moldings to stylish leaded glass chandeliers and crystal doorknobs.

The restoration was so successful that the Colonial Inn received the "People in Preservation" award from the Save Our Heritage Organization. It was said that, "the Colonial Inn... brings the very best from La Jolla's past tastefully into the present. Elegance, continental service, graceful design and décor, all embraced in the ambience of a small European hotel."

In 1980, the space once occupied by Putnam's drugstore became Putnam's Grille. Reflecting the La Jolla of the 1920s, the restaurant was redesigned to feature dark wood paneling, wrought iron chandeliers and ceiling fans, oak dining sets and large picture windows that created an open, fluid environment. The original soda fountain was replaced with a mirrored back bar and alcoholic beverages were served instead of ice cream sodas. The restaurant also stayed true to its heritage by offering diners sidewalk seating, continuing the tradition of the past sixty-five years.

Business continued to be good for the inn, and in 1988, it was sold for an estimated $13.85 million to a Japanese-based investment firm, Tokyo Masuiwaya California. In 1993, "La Jolla's jewel," as the Colonial Inn was affectionately referred to, celebrated its 80th birthday.

In July of 1998, Franklin Croft LLC and Fargo Hotel investors LLC joined forces to create Fargo Colonial LLC and purchased the hotel. Fargo Colonial LLC brought aboard hotel veteran Terry Underwood as general manager in 1999. From December 1999 through July 2001, The Grande Colonial underwent an extensive five million renovation and, under the leadership of Underwood, the hotel's guest rooms, suites, lobby and restaurant were dramatically upgraded.

Between 2007 and 2008, the hotel took another stride forward as it unveiled the completion of an $8 million restoration project, which elevated the hotel's rating to Four Diamond status. Included was the renovation of the hotel's existing guest rooms, suites and corridors in the main building, as well as replacement of the original single-pane, wood-framed windows with double-pane, screen-less, tempered glass windows significantly improving the energy efficiency, sound and insulation.

The project also included the preservation of two adjacent historic landmarks, the Little Hotel by the Sea and the Garden Terraces, adding eighteen new suites to the hotel's inventory (all with kitchens or kitchenettes and fireplaces). The eight-suite Little Hotel by the Sea and the ten-suite Garden Terraces had operated as residential apartment complexes for the past 30 years and had now been restored to their original glory for the community to enjoy for years to come. To recognize their historical significance in the development of La Jolla, both properties were designated as historic sites in 1984 and 1990 respectively.

Two significant elements of the Little Hotel by the Sea included the restoration of the building's rooftop "loft" and deck, and restoration of the 1929 Baker & Sons elevator. The rooftop is now used as a guest library and sitting room, as well as an outdoor terrace providing panoramic views of the Pacific. The Loft can also be reserved for private executive board meetings for up to eight.

The Baker & Sons elevator, which has been restored to full operation, is a four-passenger, solid-mahogany elevator housed in a steel tower. Soon after it was added to the hotel back in 1929, it became recognized as the "The Smallest Hotel in the World with an Elevator".

Just as the hotel envisioned by George Bane, The Grande Colonial La Jolla, a 2010 AAA Four Diamond Award recipient, is a classic European-style hotel that rivals anything in the West. The Grande Colonial staff strives to preserve the heritage laid down by the hotel's founders nearly a century ago by providing the most gracious experience in resort and business accommodations.

The Grande Colonial Hotel in La Jolla, California has been a part of the La Jolla landscape since 1913. It was originally an apartment hotel. It has been home to celebrities, who were looking for an ideal escape from their very public lives.

The La Jolla Playhouse, founded in 1947 by Gregory Peck, Dorothy McGuire, and Mel Ferrer, attracted several up-and-comers and many famous actors and celebrities. One guestroom in particular, was a favorite of the visiting celebrities.

With a semi-private entrance and exit, this particular room was the scene of several discrete liaisons. Celebrities wanting to keep their private life, well private, would request this room. Today, they still seem to enjoy the room. This still has its secluded entrance and exit.

The Ghost Stories

The Grande Colonial Hotel in La Jolla, California has been a part of the La Jolla landscape since 1913. It was originally an apartment hotel. It has been home to celebrities, who were looking for an ideal escape from their very public lives.

The La Jolla Playhouse, founded in 1947 by Gregory Peck, Dorothy McGuire, and Mel Ferrer, attracted several up-and-comers and many famous actors and celebrities. One guestroom in particular, was a favorite of the visiting celebrities.

With a semi-private entrance and exit, this particular room was the scene of several discrete liaisons. Celebrities wanting to keep their private life, well private, would request this room. Today, they still seem to enjoy the room. This still has its secluded entrance and exit.

Each time, an employee was dispatched to the room to make sure everything was okay. Upon checking the room, one employee saw a figure hiding behind some curtains. As he approached, the curtains fell flat.

Upon investigation of the curtains, there was no open window and no breeze to account for the movement. Perhaps they just wanted some room service!

*****

A tall gentleman in a tuxedo, top hat, white scarf, and cane was seen roaming the halls of the 1928 building one late evening.

A lady in a crème-colored evening gown accompanied him. The clerk who saw them was concerned, as he did not recognize them, and the hour was very late. He rushed after them, rounding the corner—and no one was there...

*****

The Grande Colonial Hotel has been remodeled several times. When the restaurant NINE-TEN was created, it seems the spirits were very unhappy.

Restaurant staff would leave pots of broth or sauces simmering overnight, for the next day's menu. They would return to find either the pilot lights snuffed out or the stove turned all the way up.

Doors opening and closing, items moved and strange noises were the telltale signs that they were not happy. After the remodel of the hotel was complete things did quiet down somewhat. The stoves don't seem to have the same problems today, but the noises and door opening and closing still occur in the bakery. Perhaps they are just after some of our scrumptious desserts...

*****

The North Annex in The Grande Colonial's 1913 section is particularly active. Several guests and staff members have heard someone running very heavily and fast down from the third floor to the second floor. A swinging door separates the guest rooms from our meeting room and kitchen.

A staff member was working in the meeting room around 10:00 AM and heard a ruckus; someone was running down the stairs. She rushed to the entrance, and the swinging door opened in front of her. Nobody came through the door; it just swung closed in front of her. Not a soul (forgive the pun) in the hallway or stairs with nowhere to hide.

*****

Guests in the North Annex of The Grande Colonial Hotel sometimes complain of noises in the wee hours of the night from the guests below their rooms. Loud voices, doors slamming and heavy footsteps have been heard. The only problem is that there are no guests in those rooms.

Below is the bakery which, once upon a time, was two apartments. It seems that two men lived in one apartment and two women in the other and they often got together and had parties. It seems they enjoyed it so much that they still continue to party to this day.

The Colonial staff investigates every complaint and the outcome is always the same…the bakery is empty and locked up tight for the night.

*****

Imagine the Suites building at The Grande Colonial hotel in 1913. Ladies sitting on the front porch, visiting and sewing, enjoying the fresh, ocean air. It seems that one of these ladies has never left.

Back in the day when the hotel was new, a family and their maid stayed in one of the apartments overlooking the ocean. Now the suites' building has two staircases. The servants' staircase is very narrow and this maid was a rather large woman. In her travels up and down the stairs, it wore away the paint on the railings of the staircase.

Today, that staircase railing seems to wear away faster than the other side. It could just be coincidence, but I like to think of that dedicated lady, taking care of her family. Watching the waves from her window…

*****

Normandy Invasion at The Grande Colonial in La Jolla?

The meeting room often in question of strange happenings is the Sun Room. The Sun Room is currently a favorite for private events with its fabulous ocean view and cozy fireplace.

Sixty years ago, however, the Sun Room was used as a temporary barracks for single servicemen during WWII. Hardwood floors still exist under the carpet in the "North Annex" of The Grande Colonial. During the early part of The Grande Colonial's life, the "North Annex" and the Sun Room were not carpeted.

The historic battle known as "D-Day" occurred on June 6, 1944. Perhaps the spirits of those long ago soldiers were reliving the events on the 60th anniversary of the Normandy Invasion.

Could the noises heard perhaps be the spirits of those men preparing to join their comrades in arms across the seas?

*****

During the early morning of June 6, 2004, a guest in room #122 awoke at 3:00 AM feeling a bit odd. She lay in her bed for a few moments pondering the strange feelings, not quite sure what they were. Suddenly she heard heavy footsteps on the staircase outside of her room.

Up and down, several people ran, stomping on each step and a door was slamming repeatedly! This went on for quite a while.

She lay in her bed, covers pulled up over her head, wondering if she should dare open the door to see what was going on.

At last, she opened her door and peered out, but there was no one to be seen. She was certain she heard multiple heavy footsteps of men running up and down the stairs, and the stairs sounded hollow, as if there was no carpet on them.

Also, the "slamming door" she heard was not to a guest room at all, but to a meeting room. At 3:00 AM in the morning, it was very unlikely that there would be a meeting going on.

She notified the staff and was assured that no one used that room during the wee hours of the morning and that the security staff made regular rounds and nothing unusual had occurred. At her request, the guest was moved to another room so she could sleep a bit easier, away from the noisy ghosts.

*****

During a recent remodel of the Sun Room, employees Carla & Matt, were talking in the kitchen and observed a frying pan securely stacked on rack above lift up and set down on the counter!

*****

Another employee, Chrissy, was recently in the Sun Room and heard heavy footsteps thundering down the stairs in the North

Annex. She raced to the swinging door partition between the Sun Room and guest rooms to catch the culprit. The door swung open to meet her, but no one came through the door and the hallway/staircase was empty.

*****

On the morning of 8/5/05, a hotel guest reported to us that her son (11 years old) saw several "small Abraham Lincoln heads jumping around his room. Later the same boy awoke to find a lady with brown hair, all dressed in white, brushing his hair. They were staying in Room #320. The mother reported to us that strange phenomenon happens to them all the time.

*****

Over the weekend of 11/5/05, a guest was staying in Room #508. One night in particular, she was having difficulty sleeping. She awoke at 3:00 AM precisely and noticed a presence in the room. She described it as a "heavy feeling." Nothing menacing or intrusive…just a "curiosity," as if she were being watched. She noticed a strange, soft glow in the room. However, all of the lights were out and the shades were drawn. She saw an image of a girl, roughly twenty-three years old, with brown hair, and wearing a light lace dress.

For some reason since the incident, this hotel guest has been unable to get the name Abigail out of her head. She also thought she may have heard the name "Trent" but was unsure. This guest has never known anyone by the name of Abigail Trent in her life.

She considers herself to be a very, levelheaded nurse of ten years on her way to getting a PhD and becoming a doctor. She is not superstitious or into the supernatural. Nevertheless, now she is definitely a believer!

*****

We hear more stories every day and have recently been informed that the ghosts in the kitchen are back to playing with the stove, turning the flame up and down when no one is around.

*****

The kitchen and bakery are VERY active and so is the ladies' room. You might hear someone walking around or the doorknob turning when no one but you is in the room. It can be a little scary.

*****

One of our housekeepers said she saw faces peering out from one of the windows on the 1st floor of the suites building and was so spooked she switched to day shift!

*****

Shane Roberts, one of the desk clerks, has a story about when his parents came to visit in January, 2010.

My mother got up during the night to crack the window a little bit. After she did that, she was on the way back to the bed. She'd been kind of sick, so she couldn't find any water but happened to find a Dr. Pepper sitting on the table

She didn't turn on any lights, drank the Dr. Pepper, and got back into bed. My dad woke up a little bit; just enough to be conscious enough to know she was getting in and out of bed. After she lay back down, she heard a woman's voice say, "Are you drinking water?"

My dad didn't hear the voice. My mother did and as soon as my mom heard the voice she said, "Who said that?"

My dad rose up and realized that the lamp beside the bed was on and nobody had turned it on.

He asked, "Who turned the lamp on?"

My mom said, "Get us out of this room!"

This happened in Room #510. Just so happens that is the room number where I stayed in the next hotel that I visited...da da da da, da da da da!!

*****

The Sweets Building is very spooky. The old caretaker of the building lived there when it was originally apartments. She would walk up and down the banister. She was a heavy-set woman and would put so much weight on the banister that to this day, we have to finish that banister more than any other banister in the building.

*****

The sunroom housed Military men in WWII. There were barracks set up in there and the Red Cross set up in the lobby; they actually slept in this room, but here are some 'non-military' ghost stories that have occurred in this room. Shadows have also been seen in this room.

*****

Summer Dunsmore, *Hostess, had a spooky story to tell.*

It happened right after I had been talking to some of the servers about ghosts and stuff that happens here. It was kind of weird that it happened right after.

I had walked over to the Parlor Room, looking at the windows, and then the doors started to shake like someone was about to come out. I jumped back because I was looking at the mirror and didn't want to get hit in the face.

Nobody came, so I opened the door and all the lights were off, all the windows and the other door was closed as well. No wind was there that had shaken the doors or anything that had caused a pressure change. I was creeped out about it.

The Parlor Room itself has a foreboding presence to me. I stand right there near it all day at my workstation. When I walk in it feels emptier than other rooms. It sometimes feels like someone is watching me. It's something a little heavy even when the music is on and people are in there. It's not like the lobby with a warm and inviting presence. This happened a month ago.

I told Gloria about it. She walked me over and showed me the haunted staircase. She also told me about some other stories that people had told her.

Stories about when one of the bartenders saw someone standing in the hall and many people reporting a lot of stomping they've heard when staying on the top floor.

An employee's parents were staying here in that top room and heard stomping above them...which is impossible because it's on the top floor with no room above. Some people think that the stomping has something to do with the military.

*****

Sarah, Bartender, has seen a hanging wine glass, spinning by itself.

Chapter 2
Elkhorn Inn & Theatre

Dan and Elisse Clark
Route 52, Landgraff, WV
Tel/fax: 304-862-2031 Toll-free: 1-800-708-2040
Website: http://www.elkhorninnwv.com/

History

The story began in the summer of 2002, when Dan and Elisse found the inn and theatre. They both are employed by FEMA. Dan was working for the FEMA Disaster Recovery Operation, following the flooding of southern West Virginia in May 2002.

Driving for months through McDowell County, Dan often passed the historic "Coal Heritage Trail" building and the copy of Shakespeare's Globe Theatre. Flooded twice, abandoned, and vandalized, the inn building was a mud and mold-filled shell. The deck and bridge had been destroyed; the doors had been stolen along with just about everything else; only six claw-foot bathtubs, a few toilets and sinks remained intact.

The darling little theatre had been abandoned and water-logged. The property had been used as a dumping ground for everything from tires to broken appliances. But, Dan and Elisse looked at it and saw what it could be; an elegant inn with lovely rooms filled with art and vintage quilts.

The patio, with cafe tables, could be used for relaxing and watching trains or birds. A balcony to sip on a glass of wine as the mist covers the mountains at twilight and the "Pokey" railroad goes by with local bands playing at the theatre.

There would be a shop filled with unique West Virginia arts and crafts… artists-in-residence… meetings and special events… a lovely dining room for parties and weddings… perhaps even a small museum to showcase the history of the area… and their home.

They took leave from FEMA and moved to McDowell County to save and restore the inn and theatre and help the area recover from the economic devastation of the floods. They named their new home for the Elkhorn Creek, which runs between the inn and theatre.

There'd been four feet of water and mud in the inn, and there was five feet of mud still in the basement. So, in the middle of an ice-storm, Dan shoveled out the mud, gutted the entire first floor, and power-washed it with bleach three times.

They moved into their new home in January 2003. Dan rewired, re-plumbed, and rebuilt it from the roof down.

Ghost Stories

We had a number of very odd things happen after we moved in. We felt there was an entity there which Dan took to calling "Molly". (He said the name just "came" to him!)

*****

On numerous occasions, after turning off all the lights and going to bed, we'd find them all on in the morning, (or in the middle of the night,) after we'd been awakened by a loud bang!

*****

One morning at 7:00 AM, we were both roused by a loud "bonking" noise that sounded like two by fours being banged together. Dan ran around the building and found no one; the inn was locked up tighter than a drum!

*****

One night we heard crystal shattering, apparently at the end of the hall. We looked at each other, nodded (yes, we both had heard it,) and then ran through the building again. We systematically went from room to room, and found nothing amiss.

*****

I was at the computer (Dan was asleep) and I heard a pounding on the front door with…one heavy bang, and then bang-bang-bang! I thought someone was trying to break down the door! I woke Dan up and we both ran downstairs, only to find nothing except that every light on the second floor was on.

One painting was now laying flat on the floor, face down. I re-hung it and we turned off all the lights and went back to bed. The next day the same painting was down again, but leaning against the wall. We re-hung it, and I looked at the ceiling and said "Okay! I know you don't like that painting! Why??? What am I supposed to do?" No answer!

*****

My husband was so spooked by the feeling that someone (besides us) was in the building. He spent a night sitting in a chair in the middle of our living room! (He is US Army Retired and spooks at NOTHING!) It got to the point where lights would go on or off or things would "go bang" quite a bit. I'd simply look up at the ceiling and exclaim, "Molly, if you want me to understand what you want, write it on the bathroom mirror with my lipstick!" (I'm still waiting…)

*****

When we had three Irish roofers come to the inn to re-do our roof, they stayed for a week. One evening, they came down to dinner and one of the men told us that, although he had locked his door, he'd found it unlocked the next morning. So, the next night he made certain that he had locked it, only to find it, again, unlocked in the morning.

He then told us that while he was seated at the dresser, with his back to his room's door, it opened and a "female spirit" stood in the doorway. He said, (without turning around.) "We're just here to do the roof," at which point, "she" left! He then told us that all this was okay, because he was used to it. "This is normal in Ireland," was how he put it…

*****

Halloween came around, and as much as I looked at the ceiling and begged "Molly" to come out and play (gently) for our guests, nothing happened! For the last seven years that we've had the inn, no guest has ever mentioned anything.

*****

When Dan's sister was staying with us she said that there was a knock on her door the morning she was to leave and that someone had turned her (locked) doorknob. She assumed it was Dan and got up; except, it wasn't Dan. He was asleep in bed with me and there was no one else in the building! (Fortunately, Pat thought this was "cool!")

*****

We learned that, in the 1920s, there was supposedly a murder at the pay window on the first floor. A disgruntled miner shot the Paymaster and another coal company employee.

There was a woman, who worked in the building in the 1940s, that supposedly died in one of the offices.

*****

We have also seen a newspaper report of a woman who was hit by a train. She was a relative of a frequent guest of the inn. She was carried into the wooden building (known as "The Hotel,") that our building replaced after it burned down around the turn-of-the-century....

*****

Miguel Criado has been the inn's artist-in-resident several times. He told us that while he was staying here, he "saw" a girl in the fireplace room one night, dressed in "old-fashioned clothing;" as he described it. We realized he was describing 1900s American period dress; a long skirt, short dark boots, and dark stockings... perhaps this was a long ago worker in the building, or the lady that was hit by the train???

*****

In November 2002, when we were in the process of buying the building, we were at Miguel's house. A "psychic" friend of his, who we'd never met before, was there. We were told, "Your building has a female spirit; a woman who died in the building. She wasn't a happy person, but she means no harm.") We didn't know much about any of the "goings on" at that time.

*****

Our friend Terry, who was our house sitter last month for 2 weeks, apparently had a couple of "Molly" experiences! His two little tiny doggies, Stella & Lucky, although blocked with a dog-gate from going upstairs, managed to "somehow" get themselves locked into a variety of rooms on the 2nd and 3rd floor over and over again!

He spent 2 weeks playing "hide & go seek" and is positive it was Molly having fun with him! He also said he "felt" a woman's presence in the dining room—but that she was "shy"—nothing upsetting.

We do find it interesting that all the people who have had

"Molly" experiences were staying here without paying… (Dan's sister Pat, our artist friend Miguel, a house sitter 6 years ago, the Irish roofers, Terry…) No paying guest has ever reported a "Molly" experience…

*****

Shortly after we bought the building, Miguel told us he had a "feeling" that there was "money in the walls", but he didn't know what that meant. I immediately went around the building, tapping on our many walls, trying to find a "space" that might conceal hidden treasure, but to no avail!

I thought that might have been the wall where the painting dropped off twice, I thought that must be "the wall"—but there's no space behind it! We have yet to discover what "money in the walls" means!

So who knows, maybe this Halloween "Molly" will come out and play again! And perhaps we'll find the "money in the walls!"

Chapter 3
1859 Historic National Hotel

18183 Main Street • P.O. Box 502 • Jamestown, CA 95327
Reservations:(800) 894-3446 Fax:(209) 984-5620
Stephen Willey, Your Host since 1974
Website: http://www.national-hotel.com/

History

In 1859, Heinrich and Hannah Neilson established a hotel, bar, and restaurant that was to become known as The National Hotel. The two wooden buildings were among the first permanent structures in this early (1848) gold rush town of Jamestown. The National Hotel has been in continuous operation from this date, having survived two damaging fires in 1901 and 1927. It then had to be remodeled.

Today's restoration work was begun in 1974 by present owners and has been ongoing some 35 years later.

In August of 1974, The National Hotel was purchased by present owners Stephen Willey and his brother Michel Willey. While the bar and hotel had functioned continuously from its beginning, the restaurant was not open, and had not been fully utilized since 1946. With limited funds, and providing the labor themselves, the restaurant was reopened in September 1975.

Flo

Our resident ghost, Flo, is a friendly ghost, known for harmless pranks and mysterious

goings on. The current owner, Stephen Willey, has been hearing stories of her presence for

thirty-five years.

*****

Flo generally stays upstairs in the hotel, seemingly favoring the rooms in the front of the building although she has been seen in each of the rooms, and on occasion, been seen early in the morning downstairs, floating through the dining room and right through the walls!

*****

Each of our guest rooms has a notebook which welcomes guests to share their experiences and comments. There are numerous accounts of doors slamming, lights going on and off, clothing being dumped from suitcases onto the floor, and a woman's sobbing coming from the hallway in the middle of the night.

Whoever she is, she adds a little extra spice to all our lives. Many a non-believer has left here with a whole new attitude. Our housekeepers say they have gone into rooms only to be greeted by icy cold air, even though the heater was working.

*****

Back in the late 1800s, when Jamestown was a bustling enclave in the prosperous heart of the Gold Country, a striking young woman stepped off the train and checked into a cozy room at the Historic National Hotel. Time has erased her surname, but "old timers" remembered hearing her first name as "Flora" and guessed her age to be around 19.

According to historians of Gold Rush history, sheriff reports, and witness accounts have became local lore, we have a sketch of her story.

Flora, later known as "Flo" made mention to fellow hotel guests that she had been raised by her grandmother, a wealthy woman on the East Coast. After her grandmother died, she left New York and embarked on a trip to live with a relative in San Francisco.

On the train trip westward, she met a dark-haired, handsome young lawyer named Henry, who worked for a group of San Francisco mining investors. It was love at first sight, and by the time they reached California, Henry had proposed marriage. Knowing her relatives would be outraged, they made plans to meet six weeks later in Jamestown, where Henry often traveled on business, to be wed. He had grown to love this area, and had a particular fondness for The National Hotel.

So, after a short stay with her relatives, Flo secretly boarded the train for the trip east into the rolling foothills. She arrived in Jamestown, in a state of happy anticipation, again staying at the National Hotel. Details of her stay are sketchy, but we do know that the bride-to-be met her future husband with a joyous embrace at the train depot a few days before Christmas and immediately hired a local dressmaker to sew a lovely, lace-trimmed wedding gown.

Of course, they stayed in separate rooms and met for breakfast each morning to plan their wedding. On Christmas day, Henry presented Flo with a beautiful diamond ring. The day after Christmas, Flo was waiting for Henry to come down when she heard a shot ring out.

By some accounts, what happened next was a crime, although no one was ever caught or prosecuted; in others, it appears a tragic accident involving a town drunk. The accounts are vague, but all agree on one point; on the sometimes rough streets of Jamestown, a drunken young man stumbled into the front doorway of National Hotel and shot Henry as he descended the stairs from the rooms above.

In the cold air of that December morning, Flo ran to find Henry lying at the bottom of the stairs in a pool of blood by the open door. The hotel staff heard uncontrollable sobs throughout that sad day and night, and the next night, and the next. Then, on New Year's Eve…silence.

Alarmed by Flo's sudden silence, hotel staff entered her room and inside they found the young woman, dressed in the lace-trimmed wedding gown, with no breath coming from her lips, neatly seated in a chair at the open window. Cause of death was recorded as heart failure, but those who bore witness to her loss knew that a heart had not failed—it had been broken. Revelers later told of seeing a floating "woman in white" in an upstairs window as they staggered past the hotel that night.

As sad as those long ago events were, tragedy does not seem to be part of Flo's modern-day persona. However, she is a bit of a mischief-maker.

Some of our visitors, invited to share their thoughts in journals kept in each room, have reported doors slamming, lights flickering, and items tossed from suitcases and shelves.

*****

Our staff has also witnessed the other-worldly shenanigans. Chefs have reported pans tumbling off shelves, and spoons and ladles suddenly swinging wildly from wall hooks. Guests tell of entering their rooms to find the heater unexpectedly on and the room warm, yet feeling an icy blast of air brush past them into the hallway.

*****

For the most part, though, Flo is a cheerful presence who seems intent on a long and happy stay—a fate we wish for all our guests.

As for what keeps her here, we can only guess she is here with her memories of her beloved Henry. Perhaps for Flo, The National Hotel and the beautiful plans of that Holiday season long ago, are simply too dear to leave behind.

If you happen to see Flo, please say hello and wish her well. As a point of interest, she seems to favor the second story rooms, but on occasion has been seen downstairs in the pre-dawn hours—floating through the dining room walls.

Perhaps some loves are too strong to fade in the course of a mere century.

Chapter 4
St. Francis Inn

279 St. George Street, St. Augustine, Florida 32084
Toll-free: 1-800-824-6062
Tel: (904) 824-6068 • Fax: (904) 810-5525
Email: info@stfrancisinn.com

Website: http://www.stfrancisinn.com/

History

Just around the corner from St. Augustine's picturesque "Oldest House," you'll find what is unquestionably St. Augustine's "oldest inn;" the St. Francis. Dating from 1791, the inn embodies the rich history and culture of the nation's oldest city, and visitors are invited to delve into the stories that comprise its colorful past.

The inn dates from the city's Second Spanish Colonial Period; its architecture reflects the early residents' concern for their own safety and protection. So great was the threat of invasion that, by order of the King of Spain, houses were to be constructed so that they might "serve as a defense of fortress against those who might attempt to occupy the town." Consequently, the building stands directly on the street, shielding the front entrance and peaceful courtyard enjoyed by visitors and residents alike.

Gaspar Garcia, the property's first owner, was a military man. A sergeant in the Third Battalion of the Infantry Regiment of Cuba, he was granted the lot in 1791 by the King of Spain, and shortly thereafter built a home. In 1802, the property was purchased by Juan Ruggiers, a sea captain, whose family held it until the early years of American rule in Florida.

Subsequent owners and residents included other military figures. In 1838 it became the property of Colonel Thomas Henry Dummett. Dummett, who grew up on the Caribbean island of Barbados, retired from Britain's Royal marines and began a sugar plantation. He and his wife Mary had eleven children, however only six lived to adulthood. And only three—son Douglas and daughters Anna Maria and Mary Mortimer—lived to see middle age.

In 1819, Dummett had moved his family to America after the English ban on slave trade caused many planters in the colonies to give up their way of life. There is a story that British authorities tried to detain Dummett and that he smuggled himself aboard a ship, hiding in an empty sugar barrel.

In 1825, Dummett bought several hundred acres along the Tomoka River south of St. Augustine and built a sugar mill plantation. After a few years of struggling, and developing a rum distillery to process some of his crop, Dummett began to prosper. Like other well-to-do planters, Dummett kept a house in St. Augustine, now the St. Francis Inn.

Carrying on the military tradition, Colonel Dummett's daughter Elizabeth married William J. Hardee, an 1838 graduate of West Point and survivor of the battles of Shiloh, Missionary Ridge, and Atlanta. His Rifle and Light Infantry Tactics was adopted as a textbook for the Army. Another Dummett daughter married Brigadier General Melville A. Cochran, whose book of reminiscences described the inn as "one of the best in St. Augustine" at the time of the Civil War.

After Colonel Dummett's death, his daughter Anna, who never married, converted the family home into a lodging establishment in 1845. Anna raised ten nieces and nephews—children of three of her sisters who had died before the 1860s.

When Florida seceded from the Union in 1861, Anna embraced the Confederate cause, even though St. Augustine was quickly occupied by Northern troops and remained under Yankee control until peace came in 1865. After the war, Anna led a drive to collect money for a monument to the Confederate dead. The monument, an obelisk, still stands in St. Augustine's central plaza.

Anna lived until 1899, but she left memoirs of her childhood on the plantation. Sub-tropical forest has reclaimed her father's Florida sugar plantation, but jumbled piles of brick, two stone arches and two tall coquina chimneys can be seen at the ruins, just off Old Dixie Highway, about a mile and a half north of the bridge over the Tomoka River in Ormond.

A prominent philanthropist named John L. Wilson purchased the inn in 1888. Along with extensive renovations to the inn (such as adding the third floor and mansard roof), he was responsible for a number of new buildings in the neighboring area. Wilson designed and built a house at 34 St. Francis Street which is currently occupied by our innkeepers and their family.

Later Mr. Wilson built the house at 280 St. George Street for his daughter Emily. This house, which we call the Wilson House, now includes four rooms and suites of St. Francis Inn. Wilson also donated the first public library, on Aviles Street, on the one condition that Emily Wilson be the librarian!

It should be noted that the inn was not always named "St. Francis." During the first twenty years of this century, the building was identified as "The Teahan House," "The Hudson House," "The Valencia Annex," (named after the Valencia Hotel which was located on the side of our current parking lot,) "The Amity Apartments," "The Salt Air Apartments," "The Palms," and "The Graham House" It was not until 1948 that the inn was christened "The St. Francis Inn.

The Ghosts

St. Augustine, being America's oldest city, has a colorful history of four centuries and many legends of ghostly figures. Some believe that the ghost of a young house servant haunts St. Francis Inn. She has become known as "Lily" and strange happenings reported in one third floor inn room lead to it being named "Lily's Room."

*****

This is the story of one of the most interesting and recent stories that happened at our inn about a year ago. A gentleman, who has done a lot of construction and renovation work on the inn, was doing some work in the bathroom of one of our suites on the third floor. He looked out into the bedroom and saw a housekeeper making up the bed. (The third floor is the most active area of the inn,) although our ghost does do things all over the inn.

He acknowledged her, she acknowledged him and he said something to her about not worrying about the mess, he would clean it up; he's notorious for leaving things in a mess.

When he finished he went downstairs and spoke to the innkeeper and said, "So, you have a new housekeeper."

The innkeeper said, "No, we don't have a new housekeeper. We have the same crew that has worked here for a long time.

"No, I just saw a black lady working in the Garcia suite.

Our innkeeper repeated that we didn't have a new one and we don't have a black housekeeper here at all.

41

So, of course they both ran upstairs and...no black housekeeper. However, the bed was all made up. (Our housekeepers had not been to that room yet.)

This story is a very credible story since this fellow knows the inn and is not the type of person that would do this as a prank...this really happened to him.

*****

A story is told of a young man who lived with his uncle, Major William Hardee, who owned the inn during the middle of the 19th century. He fell in love with "Lily," one of the young black servant girls, believed to have been a beautiful slave woman from Barbados, and they would sneak into rooms of the inn to carry on their secret love affair.

When the uncle, a military officer, walked in on the lovers he dismissed the servant and ordered his nephew to never see her again. The nephew, deeply depressed, killed himself. Some say by hanging himself in the attic, now Lily's Room, others say by jumping from the third floor window.

*****

For years, inn guests and employees have reported apparitions of the ghost in Lily's Room and in other parts of the inn. Some have seen her passing in the hall, all dressed in white. Maybe she returns to find her lover.

*****

One housekeeper tells of listening to MTV on the television while cleaning Lily's Room. When she returned from getting clean sheets in the hall, the television was turned off. She jokes "Lily didn't like MTV!"

*****

Interesting phenomena has been reported by guests about Lily and her soldier lover. A woman staying in Lily's Room was awakened by a loud noise and woke to find the contents of her pocketbook scattered across the floor. Nothing was missing and she said the thud was too loud to have been merely the sound of the purse falling.

*****

A guest found her cosmetic bag full of water, while another found her makeup bag under an open window. It had stayed completely dry while the driving rain had soaked everything around it.

*****

A male guest found himself under the bed when he woke in the morning, and had to get help to free himself.

*****

In another occurrence, a new bride was awakened by a passionate kiss, and then surprised to find her husband was sleeping soundly beside her.

*****

Other reports include sightings of a hand on the railing of the back stairs, a ghostly figure dressed in white passing in the halls. Split-second sightings of spirits and frequent sounds of whispers and moans have been heard as well as lights and coffee makers going on and off unassisted. Radio stations are changed as witnesses' watch, locked doors are found open, and shower water comes out hotter and hotter no matter how much cold is added.

Other instances include falling books, moving pictures, icy cold touches, covers being removed, and female and male apparitions. Some psychics, who have been to the inn, conclude that Lily and her lover have not been united in the afterlife within the inn they haunt.

*****

Was it the resident ghost who caused a disturbing evening for another guest? He and his wife were staying at the inn, but in a room other than Lily's Room. His wife fell asleep quickly, but he had trouble. A strange sensation overcame him suddenly, which he said felt like someone was entering his consciousness, without seeming to be either good or evil.

He left the room to see if a short walk would help, and then returned to bed only to have the same feeling, and he attempted to allow it to become stronger. After what he thought was a long time, he shook off the feeling and went for another walk and some coffee, finally returning to the room and able to fall asleep.

*****

Fortunately, the recalled paranormal events at St. Francis Inn have been described as friendly, though sometimes mischievous, but not harmful. Many describe their apparitions as being pleasant, not disturbing. Many guests are attracted by the possibility of a ghostly encounter.

Chapter 5
Thaddeus Clapp House

74 Wendell Avenue—Pittsfield, Massachusetts (MA) 01201
Toll Free: 888-499-6840—Phone: 413-499-6840
FAX: 413-499-6842
Rebecca Smith, Owner
Email: info@clapphouse.comWebsite: www.clapphouse.com

History

According to the Berkshire County Historical Society, "Taxes were the motivation for the founding of Pittsfield. In 1735, the city of Boston, complaining that its tax burden was unfair, petitioned the general court for a grant of deeds in western Massachusetts that it could then resell to earn revenue."

Boston native, Jacob Wendell, surveyed the area, and then called Poontoosuck, which was Mohegan meaning "land of the winter deer." The result was the creation of two major roads (now East-West and North-South) and 60 building sites. In 1761, the town was incorporated and renamed Pittsfield in honor of the English Prime Minister, William Pitt, who was considered a friend of the Colonies. Jacob Wendell moved his family to Pittsfield and settled in the community.

Slightly to the east of the intersection of North, South, East and West Streets, the area known as Park Square was created. By 1829, public sidewalks and many beautiful churches and public buildings lined Park Square. Pittsfield was selected as the "county seat" for Berkshire County. In 1868, the city started the building of the county courthouse on the southeast side of Park Square at the entrance of Wendell Avenue, named for Jacob Wendell.

The Clapps attended St. Stephen Episcopal Church, re-built in 1890 on the north side of Park Square.

By the 1800's Pittsfield was the center of industry in Berkshire County. The railroad had been built and transported the products of the many textile and paper mills. Besides the many mills, Pittsfield was the location of the Stanley Electric Company. William Stanley invented the first alternating current electrical transformer. His company was bought by the General Electric Company and remained a major employer until end of the 20th Century.

But it was the railroad that opened Pittsfield to the world. Trains brought visitors from all over to the Berkshires. Many of America's wealthiest families built "cottages" throughout the county, including many in Pittsfield. One of the most well known was "The Court" built for the family which owned the Kimball Piano Company. It became Hillcrest Hospital in 1951.

Susan Eisley, Executive Director of the Berkshire County Historical Society, wrote in Pittsfield, Images of America:"Pittsfield can be an enigma. The largest and most industrial town in a county that prides itself on being 'America's Premier Cultural Resort', it has a personality that sets it quite apart from other towns. When you look closely, Pittsfield has contributed every bit as much to culture, beauty, grandeur, compassion, invention and humor as any town in the Berkshires. Without the heartbeat of the city, the county would be so much less than the wonderful place it is today."

Although Mr. Clapp was a respected businessman, his heart was in the arts. This house in those days was the center of the social life of the community and gained wide fame as such. The Berkshire Eagle, 1908. The Clapp's home was designed for entertaining and the couple often held musical performances and poetry and theatrical readings after elaborate dinner parties.

Both Mr. and Mrs. Clapp were noted amateur thespians. Mr. Clapp used the stage name of "Thaddeus Clappertino."

Unfortunately, Mr. Clapp did not live long enough to attend performances of such famous actors as Sarah Bernhardt and the Barrymores at the Colonial Theatre, which was built in 1903. Nor did he get to visit the new Berkshire Museum also built in 1903.

The Clapp's collection of 170 travel books and bound volumes of The Century and Scribner's magazines were donated to the Pittsfield Athenaeum, which at the time was the largest gift to the library. The Berkshire Athenaeum was built with funds donated by Thomas Allen, grandson of Pittsfield's famous minister, "The Fighting Rev. Allen," was well known for keeping a loaded musket close by during the Revolutionary War. The building housing the athenaeum became the Berkshire County Registry of Deeds after a new library building was built on the land between Wendell Avenue and Bartlett Street in 1967.

One of the Clapps' famous contemporaries in Pittsfield was Oliver Wendell Holmes; poet, dean of the Harvard Medical School and the great-grandson of Jacob Wendell. (Mr. Holmes is known for being the father of Oliver Wendell Holmes, Jr., who became a U.S. Supreme Court Justice.)

Another neighbor on nearby Holmes Road was Herman Melville, one of America's most celebrated authors. According to the Berkshire County Historical Society. "Herman Melville" spent many summers in Pittsfield visiting his uncle's farm (on South Street).

In 1850, he decided to move to Pittsfield permanently, buying a home that he named for the artifacts he dug up while plowing. It was at Arrowhead that Melville wrote Moby Dick along with three more novels; sixteen short stories and one volume of poetry. Many of his stories and poems were set in the Berkshires, including several set at Arrowhead. "A great neighborhood for authors, you see, is Pittsfield,' Melville wrote in 1851."

John and Sara Morewood purchased Melville's uncle's farm on South Street in 1850. Later the property became the Pittsfield Country Club. Mrs. Morewood was well known for her humanitarian work during the Civil War. Sara's son, William, married Herman Melville's niece, Maria, and they lived at Arrowhead.

Pittsfield has some of the most beautiful and historic architecture as in any city in New England. Like Wendell Avenue, many of the city's streets are named after the well-known authors, industrialists and civic leaders who built their homes in the city.

Mr. Clapp died in 1890. A few years later, Mrs. Clapp became ill and she moved to a smaller home on Henry Street. Mrs. Clapp died in 1908. Her daughter, Agnes Margaret, who married Louis Emil Berger of Brooklyn, New York, survived her. Daughter, Lillian, who was married to the Rev. William Prail of New York, died in childbirth several years before Mr. Clapp's death. Son, Theodore Harold, died in 1893 in Bermuda.

Mrs. Clapp had deeded the house on Wendell to grandson Stuart Clapp, who lived on Bartlett Street. In 1906, he sold the home to William Whittlesay. Mr. Whittlesay was a former Massachusetts senator and superintendent of the Pittsfield Electric Company.

The Whittlesays sold the home to William Wyman in 1920. Mr. Wyman was the president of the Berkshire Life Insurance Company. The company's headquarters was located across from

Park Square. The company's headquarters were later moved to another location on South Street.

In 1930, the grand home that the Clapp's lived and entertained in was converted to apartments.

Walking down Wendell Avenue and on the adjacent streets of Bartlett and Pomeroy as they intersect East Street and Park Square, one appreciates the elegance of the homes that still remain. Many are still single-family homes while others have been converted into professional offices or broken up into apartments. They have been preserved to illustrate a time long gone by.

In 1981, the Clapp House was nominated to the Massachusetts Historic Commission's Register of Historic Homes. The home was named to the National Register of Historic Places of the U.S. Department of the Interior in 1991.

Ghost Stories

The following is an interview that Rebecca gave Peter Bergman...with it the permission to quote and use in my book.

The next time someone tells you that the Berkshires is a region filled with historic homes, smile, nod and ask them how many ghosts they've slept with in those consequential dwellings. Some will laugh, others giggle nervously. A few will give you an odd look, a distorted grin and still others will turn away from you for a moment, then turn back, nod and say something like, "That never happened to me!"

*****

The house we lived in, deep in the woods off a back road in Richmond, was definitely haunted. Windows we closed would be open in the morning; footprints would appear on the porch or in the snow just outside the front steps.

*****

Noises can be heard occasionally deep in the walls that were not traceable to animals or to the settling of a nearly hundred-year-old structure.

*****

Once there was a smell of perfume—lightly lilac and something else I couldn't define—that came, stayed a full day, and then disappeared.

*****

The house we live in now, only seventy-five years old, seems gentler, quieter, but sometimes lights come on after they've been shut off for the night. Sometimes the dog is restless and uneasy for no reason.

*****

Some guests claim to have heard piano playing in the Allen Suite at 3:00 AM and some have sung along with one of the "ladies" in the Pomeroy Suite.

*****

Older houses are like that. They just are. And some of them are now active inns or bed and breakfast establishments and a few are turning this "other-world" phenomenon into a selling point.

While the house was being renovated, Smith commissioned Peter Bergman to write and direct a play to be performed in the house during its first winter open to the public, as a way to reintroduce the home to locals. The play was written so as to take its audience through seven of the suites and the three public areas on the first floor. It was during the rehearsals for this play that the Clapp House ghost first appeared.

*****

The month was December. Sally Filkins and Charlie Wright, playing Mr. and Mrs. Clapp, were rehearsing in the music room, now the breakfast room at the B & B.

This room had been built with a stage that the Clapps and their friends used for informal performances of the local theater troupe; The Williams Street Varieties. Smith had announced that she was going out and that the actors and I had the house all to ourselves. There were no guests or no day help in the building.

About twenty minutes later we heard someone on the stairs and before we could investigate, we saw a dark-haired woman in a long red coat pass through the foyer and exit the building. We assumed that this was Smith going out and thought little about it.

Not ten minutes after that, we heard the front door open again and, turning, saw the same red coat, collar up, coming into the foyer. We called out to Smith and got no reply. So, all three of us moved to the doorway of the music room, to see if she needed help. There was no one in the foyer. A moment later we heard a door slam on an upper floor.

We returned to work and within minutes the door to Smith's private quarters opened and she appeared. I turned to Becky Smith and asked her how she had managed to go upstairs and then appear so quickly downstairs. She seemed confused by the question.

We all told her about seeing a woman go out and come back. She informed us that she had gone out the back door of the house and had just come back in, the same way. She didn't own a red coat. Furthermore, her hair is blonde.

We went on a search of the upstairs suites, but there was no one in the house and nothing at all in that particular, bright shade of red.

That one incident was all there was to the haunting in 2002.

*****

Then came December, 2003...

Classical singer Amy Goldstein and her husband, composer Jonathan Faiman, were guests at the Clapp House. From the minute they entered the premises, Goldstein, who is also a professional Tarot card reader, felt something happening.

"I've stayed in upward of fifty B & Bs over the past twelve to fifteen years," Goldstein told me recently in a telephone interview, "and I've never had an experience like this one at the Clapp House."

I walked into the house, saw the large round table in the foyer and immediately noticed a ton of people walking around me, going up and coming down the stairs.

They were dressed in green, sort of a forest or dark pea green and red coats. After I was told about the Clapp family, I realized they were all family. They seemed so happy, walking with a light gait.

I said to Jonathan, "We're not the only people here. I see all these people walking around. It's freaking me out. It's not a bad feeling but no one has left this house. "

Goldstein's psychic senses were put to the test in the Clapp House and her conclusions were that this particular season, a time when the large and extended Clapp family would have been in residence or constantly visiting, was a time that no one in that family wanted to see come to an end.

"I felt the liveliness of the house," she said. "I felt strongly that the time we were there was a favorite time for that family, through the bustle in the foyer and on the stairs. One spot where I felt it considerably strong was near the back door and the corridor from the foyer. I felt a lot of action there. When I went near that door, it was cold, very different from the rest of house."

"When you know there's a person or spirit there, you realize that they have brought the season with them into that part of the house. That was the cold I felt. It wasn't bad; it was just the memory of a terribly cold winter."

Goldstein and Faiman remained guests in the house for almost a week; during that time, little changed.

"I didn't see people in the foyer so much," Goldstein laughed, "but I passed them on the stairs all the time. I kept saying 'hello' to people Jonathan couldn't see.

I'm used to paranormal experiences. It was very benevolent, nothing malicious. There was one man that I knew was the father. Becky finally described Thaddeus Clapp to me and it was him. There was a lovely looking woman, in red, which had a very casual manner. I think it was Mrs. Clapp.

"In my room, the Theodore Pomeroy Suite, I felt the buzz of people having been there, which is something I have never felt in another B&B. It was simply alive with tremendous family joy."

*****

Smith also noted a Christmas peculiarity about the house.

"We decorate, of course, and it gets very festive and Victorian in here," she said, gesturing towards the front parlor. "Then something else happens. The rooms start to take on a glow, a polished look that has nothing to do with how we clean it, or even the Christmas lights. It's like the front parlor, where Mr. Clapp died, changes somehow; as though the house really likes being decorated and somehow reacts to it. When we take down the decorations, the whole house feels sad, almost melancholy, for a while."

*****

Other guests have commented to her about hot spots and cold spots, something she herself has never experienced in this house. Room #6, with its private sun porch, had been Mrs. Clapp's room. Now it is the Theodore Pomeroy Suite.

"People sometimes report extra heat in that room," Smith

said. "Others find that room four is very comfy. It's nothing discernible but they just seem to like being in there.

That was Mr. Clapp's room and he hated to leave it." Now, that room is the Oliver Wendell Holmes Suite.

*****

Smith has done a great deal of research on the house, the people and the period. Much of that has been translated into her choices for the house, which had been a boarding house and an apartment house for awhile.

"I think I know what it must have felt like for Lucy, living here, and having to leave it," Smith commented. "She died in a house on Henry Street. The December ghost, that your actors and Amy Goldstein saw, the woman in the red coat, I think is Lucy. I think she comes back here where Thaddeus died, to be with him at the holidays."

Whether the ghost in red is Mrs. Clapp or someone else, she seems to be a real, non-threatening presence, in that house.

Talking to other B&B owners and innkeepers it becomes clear that this sort of spiritual link with the past is not uncommon in our community and in the Berkshires, it seems, a haunted house makes a comfortable home.

Chapter 6
Thayer's Historic Bed n' Breakfast

60 West Elm St
PO Box 246
Annandale, MN 55302
800-944-6595
Owner, Sharon Gammell: slg@thayers.net
Website: **http://www.thayers.net**

Owner, Sharon Gammell is an internationally trusted psychic, exceptional hostess, a talented chef and Wedding Officiate!

History
Albert Augustus Thayer, affectionately known as "Gus" to his family and friends, was born in Adrian, Michigan, on December 28, 1848 to parents who were farmers. Gus' forefathers migrated from England, coming to this country on the Mayflower.

Gus Thayer was an entrepreneur, restless and always seeking new things to do. At age sixteen, he fibbed about his age and joined C. C., of the Seventh Volunteer Infantry as a drummer boy, to get in on the excitement of the Civil War.

It was in 1878; Gus married his second wife, Miss Caroline

Hill, born in Tioga County, Pennsylvania. She came to Monticello, Minnesota with her parents, Horance and Eliza Hill, met Gus. The same year they were married, they moved to Fair Haven, Minnesota.

Gus often leaves good luck pennies for our guests.

Caroline Hill Thayer—Thayer's "First Lady"

The Thayer's resided in Fair Haven, Minnesota until 1889, when Gus got restless again and they moved on to Annandale, Minnesota. Caroline and Gus had five children together: Elaine, Effie, Bert, Martha and Agnes.

In Annandale, Gus and Caroline were offered the job as managers of the "Annandale House." Gus' official title was "Landlord," as managers of this kind of property were called. At the time there were two hotels in Annandale.

Caroline's picture hangs in the game room. And, yes, it changes!!! When she is pleased with what's happening here at Thayer's she has a wide, happy smile!

Ghosts Reside at Thayer's

Yes, Thayer's is haunted; ranked #5 on Odd Inns list of Best Haunted Places to stay in the USA. The ghosts at Thayer's are not Casper, but, they are friendly. All the same, they do like to play with people and enjoy a good boo now and again. None of the ghosts are stuck entities and visit for many reasons.

They visit because they have a great time here and come back often. They may have friends and family in the area or they may know someone that lived here or worked on the building. Someone may have even referred them. There are strong ties to the building's architecture or they may be just plain curious. They might have ridden by as a child, remembered it and wanted to visit...they may have done just that.

*****

Many photos have been taken of Thayer's ghosts; many orbs have been seen. One of the more frequent ghost guests—Miss Lilly—even helps out during Ghost Hunting 101 classes that owner Sharon Gammell offers.

*****

Ghost Kitties

Ghost Kitty, was the first of our kitties from the other side to introduce himself. He likes to sit on your bed and leaves an indentation where he has been. Some of our guests have seen him in the living room.

*****

Kimmie Cat pushes all of my papers to the floor when he thinks it's time for me to quit working. He and Clyde came to get Herald when the Professor crossed over the rainbow bridge.

*****

Clyde Kitty likes to give kitty kisses.

*****

Professor Herald purrs really loud. Last month's Ghost Hunters 101 class got a photo of our Professor Herald Kitty in Gus' room—Room #207

*****

Cocoa Bear has been seen by five guests, a number of guests have pet him, and one got a photo of him last week.

*****

New fluffy ghost kitty—A Ghost Hunters 101 guest asked me if we had a medium haired, very fluffy kitty residing here and…we do!

*****

Ghost Mouse—TN's and Miss Sadie's playmate

Chapter 7
Prospect Hill B & B Inn

Judy and Robert Hotchkiss, innkeepers and owners
801 W. Main St. | Hwy. 67
Mountain City, TN 37683
423-727-0139
Website: www.prospect-hill.com

History
Built in 1889 of hand-made brick, this house is a Victorian shingle-style home which looks very northern. Its builder, Major Joseph Wagner, served in first the Confederate, then the Union Army, during the Civil War.

He had mercantile and mining interests in the post-war era. He also served in the Tennessee legislature where he changed from a Republican to a Democrat, garnering the ire of his neighbors. This was his final home; it was sold in 1910—the year of his death.

The Rambo family bought the house in 1910 and updated it with electricity, plumbing and central heat on the first floor. Two generations of Rambos lived here. Son, Justin Rambo, arrived with his parents and was the last Rambo to live in it. It was sold at auction in August, 1991.

The buyers included the grandson of A.P Carter, known for recording the Bristol sessions—the first country music recordings. Buyer Michael Cornett is thought to have discovered the talent in a young Johnson City man—Kenny Chesney. The Cornett's, in turn, sold it to Robert and Judy Hotchkiss of Atlanta, who came looking for a house naturally suited to be a B&B.

The couple bought the house because its commanding presence on a hill makes it look like it should be a B&B and the floor plan which was readily adapted to a five-room B&B with all private baths.

Judy and Robert Hotchkiss have been renovators since one day in 1972 when they repainted door trim in an old house they rented in the Seattle area. Since then they have revived a series of turn-of-the-century homes in the Inman Park historic area of Atlanta, but nothing as daunting as a 6,000 square-foot architect-designed home located in a small town in rural Northeast Tennessee.

Robert holds a physics degree from Georgia Tech. and a law degree from Emory University. He also trained in nuclear submarines. Judy holds a journalism degree and is an avid student of renovation and gardening.

Robert and Judy completed 18-month-long initial massive renovation and remodeling just after moving in. At that point it was ready to become Prospect Hill B&B Inn, named for Major Wagner's mining interests in the area. The couple also got involved with community projects such as the renovation and reopening of the old high school auditorium as Heritage Hall Theatre and Johnson County Champion Community Board, an economic development non-profit which works to better what is one of Tennessee's most isolated and poor counties.

Five bedrooms and a two-room family parlor were turned into five guest bedrooms with modern baths. The somewhat finished attic was converted to private space for the owners. Eventually, all the hardwood floors will be lightly sanded and re-varnished. All the moldings in the public rooms were stripped of six coats of paint.

Renovation and repairs continue to this day, from details such finishes on the handmade wood moldings to a new metal, historically accurate shingle roof, gardens for wedding ceremonies and retaining walls to tame the hill and add parking space. The entire plumbing and electrical systems are new. Central heat and air conditioning were installed on the second and third floors for the first time. Six bathrooms and a new kitchen were added along with a 1500 square-foot party room, office, kitchen and public restrooms was added

Ghost stories
Told by Judy Hotchkiss

We have had several experiences ourselves. I have felt energy fields in the upstairs back hall, while in my own bed. My room is a floor above and twenty-five feet or more to the back of the house. I've heard the back door open and close when nobody is home but me! (Former owners said that they experienced the same thing.)

*****

I have heard footsteps on the front stairs and walking around the second floor hall when I was the only one inside the inn.

*****

Room #1

The guest was taking a whirlpool bath in mid-afternoon with his girlfriend just outside their door on the porch swing.

As he toweled off, he smelled spilled bourbon. He rushed to dress and find his girlfriend, who also smelled it. The odor lasted for several minutes, and then dissipated. We consider this one most reliable story because they had not been sleeping OR drinking.

Another guest of room #1, who generally can feel spirits everywhere he visits, sensed a woman's presence in this room. Circumstances only allowed this man to look into the room briefly, but he got a strong vibe right away.

*****

Room #2

One guest said she had survived near death in a traffic accident where she lost limbs and later underwent many surgeries. As she rode up the drive to check in at the inn she said that she saw a man in Civil War garb in the Room #2 window. She says that she sees ghosts of the dead whenever she is.

*****

A guest from Virginia awoke about 2:30 a.m. and smelled peanut butter cookies or muffins cooking. He thought to himself, "Wow, breakfast will be great!" Trouble is, the inn does NOT cook in the middle of the night!

*****

A couple, who enjoy pantomime as a hobby, when not staying at Bed and Breakfasts, was taking pictures of each other in their room one evening.

The first photo of the man reading on the bed was unremarkable. So was the third photo of one area of the room. However, photo #2 showed big tongues of fire leaping out of the gas log fireplace.

This MIGHT have been an electronics issue since digital cameras sometimes see things such as heat and fumes from the gas logs in odd ways. However, the innkeepers never had it happen while photographing the rooms for their website.

*****

Room #4

A guest, who generally sees spirits often, was occupying Room #4. In the middle of the night, a man in "old-fashioned clothing" came and sat in the chair at the foot of his bed.

He told the spirit. "Go away and let me at least get a good night's sleep."

It did.

*****

Room #5

Guests have heard the back door open and close. Just the same as the one-time sitter who occupied the house before it was sold at auction in 1991. Several have also heard a baby crying.

This room has the first owner's wife's initials etched in the bathroom glass. This may be where Maj. Wagner died.

Which rooms are the most haunted? I'd have to say Room #4. It used to be a nursery. But, all the others have had some sort of incident.

*****

In the Garden Area

A couple who married at the inn had parked their car on the lower apron along with friends' cars, all so it would be easy to drive to their reception site.

The first photo the innkeeper took of them walking down the drive was normal. So was the third. The second one is filled with orbs.

*****

Room #3

One business guest traveled to Mountain City from the west coast rather often. She said her last night in the inn was the scariest.

First, she heard footsteps on the grand front stairs then, there was a knock on her door at 2:30 AM....was it the cat or a ghost?

Then, the ceiling fan whirred faster and faster, energy pressed her onto the bed and refused to let her move. She tried to cry out but could not. She was stuck there for about fifteen seconds until is all subsided. This guest was facing many issues at her job. Still, when another female guest about the same age had a "dream" or incident when she awakened at night and could not move. It does make you wonder!

Chapter 8
The Village Inn Bed and Breakfast

992 Ridge Avenue
Stone Mountain, Georgia 30083
(770)469-3459 (800)214-8385 (770)469-1051 FAX
Website: http://www.villageinnbb.com/

History

The Village Inn was built in the 1820s as a roadside inn and is the oldest structure in Historic Stone Mountain Village.

The inn survived Sherman's fiery torch because of its use of a Confederate hospital during the Civil War. If these walls could talk...what stories they would have to tell.

Many mischievous things were reported during the renovation of the inn; things moving
and being turned upside down, etc. These things continued after the renovation.

Ghost Stories
Told by J. Ashley Anderson, Innkeeper

In the third floor ballroom suite, a guest heard children giggling and running across the floor. This has been reported several times. Funny though, there were no children in the inn at the times of these reports.

*****

Footsteps late at night have been reported on numerous occasions.

*****

Bathroom doors close and lock all by themselves

*****

Earlier reports include Negro spirituals being sung late at night.

*****

Some glimpse a young girl on the second floor. It was supposed that she was looking for the soldiers she had nursed during the Civil War when the inn was used as a hospital.

Chapter 9
The Historic Santa Maria Inn

801 South Broadway
Santa Maria, California (CA) 93454

Reservations: 800-462-4276 Phone: 805-928-7777 Fax: 805-928-5690
Email: innkeeper@santamariainn.com
Website: http://www.santamariainn.com/

History
In 1904, Frank J. McCoy came to Valley to work for the new Union Sugar plant in the city of Betteravia, just west of Santa Maria. Immediately he saw that the city, located almost midway between Los Angeles and San Francisco, had no comfortable hotel accommodations. He envisioned a fine hotel full of tradition and comfort for the city.

McCoy demonstrated his love of flowers by having them everywhere. At first, potted plants filled the windows of the dining room. Eventually McCoy worked out a planting schedule that provided fresh-cut flowers every day of the year. All of the inn's flowers came from its own garden just a few blocks away. The inn's famous floral arrangements have been reproduced in stained glass for windows in the historical section of the inn.

In the early years, the courtyard patio hosted McCoy's first flower gardens. It evolved into a cactus garden containing many prize specimens of succulents during the '30s and '40s. The patio is still a quiet retreat of sun and shade filled with the gentle sounds of water cascading from the antique fountain which has been the backdrop to many beautiful weddings.

In 1941, McCoy added the Olde English Tap Room, designed by Edgar Cheesewright to capture the atmosphere of an old English pub with peg-plank wooden floors and rich wormwood paneling.

By this time, the inn had become the showplace of the Valley and the center of local society, as well as a retreat for the weary traveler. The Santa Maria Inn was the stopping-off place for food and lodging in the era of motorcar travel, just as it had been in the days of horse and buggy.

Many celebrities spend the night in Santa Maria. Movie executives made the inn their headquarters, while using the beautiful countryside and ocean dunes as backdrops for their films.

The old El Camino Real, widened in 1950, became the new Highway 101. Travelers no longer rode past the inn on their way through town. The golden age of the inn faded as motorists were attracted to newer chain motels. The palatial building with its warm and charming architecture closed. For several years, attempts to re-open the inn failed.

The inn was re-opened and renovated in 1981, and the six-story tower added in 1984. The ground floor became Tower Lane Shops with several retail and service business. Downstairs are the Wine Cellar and Martini Bar health and fitness facilities, and banquet rooms.

The old palm and magnolia trees, directly in front of the entrance, are reminders of the inn's floral heritage. The lavish courtyards with fountains and park-like gardens are also testament to the enduring quality of McCoy's green thumb. The grounds, replete with flowing plants, shrubs, and ferns, are as beautiful as ever, while the modern poolside cabanas and spa offers visitors yet another chance for socializing and relaxation.

In 1999, Hardy and Judy Hearn and Robert and Blanche Hollingsead purchased the hotel. These longstanding local businesspeople dedicated themselves to a major refurbishment of the inn and have completed nearly $10 million dollars in renovations since their acquisition of the property. The Inn is currently undergoing yet another renovation of the historic rooms and public areas, thereby restoring the elegance, ambiance and gracious hospitality patrons are accustomed to. From our new swimming pool, outdoor spa, specialty suites and elevators to a brand new state of the art kitchen, the owners are committed to impeccable care and attention to detail.

Robert Hollingsead, an inventor and entrepreneur, passed away on January 24, 2002. He was definitely a visionary, who put his thumbprint on the inn's history. On May 16, 2007, the Historic Santa Maria Inn celebrated its 90th birthday. This was a special time for reflection on accomplishments, changes and traditions established through the years.

The restoration of this historic landmark turned the clock back to an era alive with traditions. The lobby, the guest rooms, the Garden Room Restaurant and dining rooms are filled with warm colors and fabrics, historical photographs and original furnishings that recall a bygone era. The inn has been designated as a city historical landmark and is known officially as the Historic San Maria Inn.

Old photographs of the early inn, its gardens and McCoy are on displayed on the inn's historic coach Room, but everywhere else are small nooks filled with living history; courtyard patio, ivy-covered balconies, imported Italian fountains, and the buff-colored adobe. The legend still lives at the inn and the Historic Original Inn wing of the hotel continues to evoke its rich history.

When McCoy retired in 1915, he searched for a suitable location for his dream. He purchased the L. E. Blochman property, eight blocks south of the center of the city. In 1916, construction of the Historic Santa Maria Inn began.

Frank J. McCoy proudly opened the doors of his fine hotel with twenty-four rooms, twenty-four baths, kitchen and dining room on May 16, 1917.

Over the years the inn grew and expanded. Twelve rooms were added in 1919. Twenty-one more rooms and another dining room appeared in 1923. Another twenty-eight rooms built in 1928 brought the inn's room count up to eighty-five.

Today the inn features one hundred sixty-four rooms, including eighteen suites. The 2000 renovation entailed a total redecoration of all sleeping rooms in the quaint and cozy original inn—with all new furniture, wall coverings, floor coverings, beds, bedspreads, televisions and amenities. In 2005, a total renovation was also completed in the Tower section of the inn.

Ghost Stories

The inn, built in 1917 has, for many years, been the favorite home of ghosts. In residence the longest, are the "Sea Captain" and his mistress. Even today they both float around the halls and call Room #221 their home. We're not sure how the Captain met his death, but his mistress met a terrible fate at the hands of an assassin.

We have had several testimonies from guests who claim they would wake in the middle of the night and see her eerie figure floating at the foot of their bed.

*****

One hotel guest staying on the second floor in a Patio Suite Room, was in bed one evening when a light bulb, from a fixture above, shot out of the socket and hit the pillow; missing his head by inches.

Thinking the socket might have been a pressure socket, the fixture was checked out by a maintenance crew and it was discovered that it was not a pressure socket but a regular "screw in" type.

*****

Even weirder, is the guest who thought she was dreaming and awoke to laughter and watched silhouettes of several people, who were seemingly at a party in her room! The host of the gala affair was next to her bed staring down at her and was costumed in mid-1800s style clothing. Nearly frantic and since she had never experienced anything like this before, she immediately picked up the phone and called her cousin seeking help. While she was dialing, the images simply vanished into thin air and were never seen by her again.

*****

Guests are not the only ones visited by our Sea Captain, his mistress and other ghostly spirits. Housekeepers, in their regular inspections of the second floor rooms in the original section, have opened locked doors to find furniture mysteriously stacked in a corner, with no explanation of how it got piled up.

*****

One housekeeper had a balloon follow her while she cleaned the second floor. When she went down the staircase to clean the rooms on the first floor, the balloon followed her downstairs. Our Executive Housekeeper personally witnessed this incident.

*****

Again in Room #221, while making a bed, another housekeeper felt a touch on her shoulder. She turned, felt a cold chill and fled the property. She could not exit the hotel fast enough, never to return, even to pick up her paycheck...

*****

For years we all have heard stories of our Old English Tap Room being haunted. The jukebox or television might inadvertently turn on. Angel Bourbon, a bartender there, has heard many eerie stories through the years and is more than willing to share them when asked.

*****

Our ghosts don't stay confined to just the original section of the inn. More recently, they have become attached to the fifth floor in the Tower section. Ryan, our Night Auditor, while in an effort to get a rollaway bed for a guest, had the fifth floor storage room door open then slam shut behind him! This was followed by an icy chill filling the room. These doors do not close automatically they must be manually closed.

After delivering the bed, instead of using the stairs, which he used to get to the fifth floor, he decided to take the elevator. He found the doors already open and waiting for him. Here again the doors do not open on their own and he hadn't called for the elevator...it should have been at the lobby level waiting to be summoned.

*****

Ryan has also experienced other rather interesting phenomenon. One evening, again working on the fifth floor in the Tower, he went to exchange a clock that a guest said wasn't working. Arriving in the room, Ryan saw the hands spinning around wildly. He picked the clock up and the hands started moving forward in an orderly fashion and stopped at the exact time of day.

*****

Another night auditor has experienced, on a daily basis, the oven door in the kitchen wildly opening and closing when getting her early morning coffee.

*****

The piano, not a player piano, has been heard playing in the ballroom from behind locked doors. Chef Jacques said upon entering, he found the room empty and the music abruptly stopped.

*****

Images appearing at bedside, balloons that follow housekeepers, jukeboxes and televisions that turn themselves on, water and lights that mysteriously turn on, clocks set themselves to the correct time and rooms that suddenly turn ice cold…Does the inn have ghosts? Spend a night or two with us and you can decide for yourself.

Chapter 10
San Remo Hotel

Mason Street
San Francisco, California 94133
(415) 776-8688 (800) 352-7366

Website: http://www.sanremohotel.com/

History
One hundred years ago, after the 1906 earthquake and fire destroyed most of San Francisco; Bank of America founder A.P. Giannini constructed a new hotel at 2237 Mason Street, close to the shoreline and shipyards at the edge of North Beach.

Giannini named his sixty-two-room three-story Italianate Victorian the "New California Hotel"—an optimistic vision of San Francisco's rebirth.

Originally, immigrant Italians found refuge at the hotel and its street-level restaurant. A transient labor force was housed at the San Remo and recruited to rebuild the city. Free meals and rooms were given to many workers who assisted the city's recovery. Other guests were merchant seaman, waterfront workers, poets, journalists, and pensioners. Penniless artists paid with their paintings.

In 1922 the hotel was renamed the San Remo, after the name of a picturesque Italian town on the Gulf of Genoa and consistent with the Genoa-style meals prepared in the restaurant. Full course dinners were offered for fifty cents during the Depression. Eventually the San Remo became a North Beach neighborhood institution, one of San Francisco's last family-style eateries and watering holes where the famous and anonymous mixed with informality for much of the century. Tom and Robert Field, brothers who have owned the hotel since 1971, continue the San Remo's long tradition of comfortable lodging, reasonable rates, turn-of-the-century charm and community service. In the spirit of Giannini, the Fields offered rooms without charge to victims of the 1989 Loma Prieta Earthquake whose homes were either destroyed or damaged.

The hotel ambiance is Old World: quiet rooms without phones or TVs, Victorian heirloom furnishings and hallways lined with historic photos. Guests share bath facilities, reminiscent of European pensione-style lodging.

There are few concessions to modern times, but travelers will find dial-up and wireless Internet access in the main hallway.

With a worldwide reputation as one of the cities's enduring treasures, many international and domestic guests are return customers. The owners and staff of the century-old hotel are dedicated to providing a comfortable and memorable visit to Victorian San Francisco.

Fior d'Italia, founded in San Francisco in 1886 and America's oldest Italian restaurant, moved to the ground level of the hotel in 2005. Now two of the city's best-known Victorian-era North Beach establishments share the same building.

Ghost Stories

Phone interview given by Kenley Gaffke, General Manager

I have been General Manager for five years and have heard many stories.

*****

A retired madam stayed in Room #33 until she decided to move to another room. (I can't remember which one and do not know why.) She had gone out of business, came here, and lived for several years. She even died in the same room in the early 1980s.

There were three times where lights have come on with nobody in the room.

*****

Room #42 has the most activity. This is where an adolescent girl of twelve to fourteen years of age roams the halls. Sometimes, you can hear her knocking.

*****

Lillian Hellman lived here and her ghost still wanders the halls. She wrote several children's books and passed away in 1984 at the age of about eighty years. She was in Hollywood when she died.

Lot of writers stayed here back in the day, until the '60s, but we still get them, just not as famous.

*****

There is a shaft at end of the hall. It is 5 x 5 and goes straight down like an air vent to the outside. This is the same effect as when you open windows to get fresh air.

An adolescent girl is seen floating out of the window. We think she died in the shaft.

*****

75

Ghost hunters said that they hit a hot spot near Room #42. Like an orb on picture…there was no flash in the mirror. It was good to see that, because it lets you know that something's there.

Chapter 11
Inn at Aberdeen

3128 South State Road 2
Valparaiso, Indiana 46385
Phone: 219-465-3753 Toll Free: 866-761-3753 Fax: 219-465-9227
Email: inn@innataberdeen.com
Website: http://www.innataberdeen.com/

History

The Kankakee River Basin of which the inn and surrounding lands are a part has been a region respected for its bountiful harvests and rich trapping and hunting preserves for centuries. Flecks of flint stone found during the environmental assessment of the entire Village of Aberdeen point to the prior presence of Indians and trappers on these grounds. The most prevalent Indians in this region were the Potawatomi. The Indians and traders of yesteryear undoubtedly traversed the land and streams that we are on today enroute from the Kankakee River to our south towards the trading posts along the shores of Lake Michigan, Baillytown settled by Joseph Baille (Bailly) near present day Chesterton and, of course, Fort Dearborn established in 1803 and later to become the City of Chicago.

Valparaiso was established as a town in 1835 followed in 1836 by the establishment of Center Township in which the inn resides. The exact dating of the buttressed walls of fieldstone, brick and concrete which form the foundation and support the living area in the historic portion of the inn is not known. County records confirm the existence of the home at least as early as 1856. An original photograph of the home known recently as Timberlake Farm hangs in the inn's old entry and depicts the seven members of the John Ritter family owners of the property in the early 1900s.

John came to Porter County in 1845 at the age of seven with his twenty-five year old father, Christian. He and his mother, Barbara Dowdeli Ritter, planted 150 apple trees in the area with seeds that they had transported from Erie County in New York. John later left Porter County to serve in the Grand Army of the Republic after which he had a brief fascination with the Gold Rush out west.

He returned to the area with his wife, Sarah J. Hesser Ritter, and their five children. Two children and Sarah later passed away and John remarried to Lottie M. Bradley in 1886 and they had five children, Jay, Ruth, Lyman, Harry and Maurice. Descendants of Ruth Ann Rifler Wilson live in the Valparaiso area today.

The original house as depicted in the photograph had a full porch with the main entry into what is now the library. The north end of the home was a single story. The original back door was found as we went to cut a door for the storage room in the southwest corner of the St. Andrews Retreat Center.

A hidden ladder beneath the old entry closet floor has led some to believe that the house served as a way station for the Underground Railroad during the Civil War linking a known site in Hebron with other sites to the north. The rustic stone wall in front of the home along Indiana Route 2 still stands today with a wrought iron railing now fixed atop.

Subsequent early remodeling in the 30's and 40's added a second story on the north end (today's Dunnotar Suite), indoor plumbing (powder room and the Aberdeen Suite's bath), and the addition to the west which currently houses the Grampian Room (kitchen), office and the innkeeper's apartment has been converted into the Alloway Suite; which is a living room/ kitchenette suite with king bed and oversized Jacuzzi.

Most recently, the property was known as Timberlake Farm recalling the heavily wooded land, variety of lakes and streams, and the rich hunting area. The stable behind the inn housed horses and offered a party room after a long day of hunting or frolicking in the woods J.M. Foster Construction Company, responsible for much of the early industrial development in northwest Indiana, owned the land during most of the 1900's until it was deeded to his daughter and her husband, Irene and Johnnie Lawson, in 1971.

The property was purchased by Benchmark, Ltd., in 1994 and subsequently by John and Linda Johnson, the Inn's proprietors, in *1995*.

Ghost stories

John and Linda started hearing the stories about strange occurrences after they bought the inn. Each of the eleven guestrooms has a diary in it for people to comment on their stay. The housekeepers read what the last guest has written and document the ghostly experiences.

*****

Different people in different rooms, who didn't know the pattern of the stories, all reported the same kinds of things happening.

*****

Sara Ritter and her daughter died of an infectious disease…no tragic or mysterious deaths.

*****

Guests report seeing a little girl on the stairway in the mornings. She wears an old, English dressing gown and is very kind. These stories are consistent.

One woman was in a room by herself…had the door locked, was in the bathroom, and had things set out on the desk in the room. When she came out, the desk was a mess and a piece of jewelry was missing.

She checked the doors and they were still locked. She was the only one in the room. She couldn't figure it out so she stepped back in the bathroom then came out a little later. Everything had been put back in the original order and whatever piece of jewelry was missing was back where it belonged.

It sounds like the little girl was messing with her!

*****

A little boy, about four years old sits sat on the stairs where the little girl hangs out. His grandmother was talking to our innkeeper at the front desk and the little boy was talking to somebody and the grandmother asked who he was talking to. He said, "The little girl."

There was no little girl in the inn, which was visible anyway. The grandmother said, "There is no little girl there."

He said, "Yes, there is," as he went right back to talking to her.

*****

A fireplace in the Aberdeen Suite comes on by itself (even while housekeeping is in the suite.

*****

Jewelry and other items in guest rooms get rearranged, running noises are heard, and brief, cold drafts are felt.

*****

People feel that the home was felt to have been a stop on the Underground Railroad from Hebron to LaPorte and into Southwest Michigan.

*****

One of the innkeepers at the front desk saw an older woman and a young girl came in out of the rain and sit down in the solarium right by the front door. He assumed they were waiting on the grandfather, or father, to catch up to them.

They were sitting there talking about the house and rooms in a way that the little girl really had to have knowledge of the house really well. They had not been in the Aberdeen Suite (which is the old master bedroom) but she was describing things along the lines of somebody that had been there. She seemed quite familiar with the house

A little bit later, they got up, went outside and the innkeeper was concerned that they needed some help or something. He said he couldn't have been more than ten seconds behind them and yet when he got outside, they weren't there. No vehicles were in the parking lot and no other guests were in the inn.

*****

Paranormal investigations have picked up on a scared, old man down in the basement although he apparently liked one of the women in the group. They thought he might have been a slave. But they were convinced that there was a man in the basement along with a little girl.

The next time they came, they got a voice recording of the little girl saying her name was "Angel."

They asked for a sign and heard squeaking on the staircase; something that couldn't be duplicated by any other means.

*****

A lot of apparent evidence came from investigators. There have been many here to visit. This is one report:

Paranormal Investigator's Findings

Aberdeen Suite (original home's master bedroom) produced some minor unusual EMF (Electromagnetic Field) meter readings, but no detections on film or cassette recording.

The door opened 6" on its own as we were leaving, but at no other time, as if someone was peaking at us.

Returned to room—unable to reproduce opening, door was level, stair pressure not a factor, and no air pressure causes. We left the room and the door opened again, on its own.

Old Kitchen area: EMF readings unusual.

Old Basement: high EMF readings at base of stairs. There were psychic impressions of little girl below trap door from main floor entry closet. Noted EVP (Electronic Voice Phenomena) in this area, "We're here, you're beautiful," something said directly towards one of the researchers.

*****

Conclusion:

"After reviewing all of the evidence gathered the day of our investigation, we are considering our results to be somewhat conclusive. The EVP, minor EMF meter readings and door opening without explanation are the strongest indications of ghostly presence. I feel that there is at least one little girl ghost and at least one male presence (possibly in the basement.)

Chapter 12
Penny Farthing Inn

83 Cedar Street
St. Augustine, Florida 32084
800-395-1890—904-824-2100
info@pennyfarthinginn.net
Website: http://www.pennyfarthinginn.net/

Located in St. Augustine's historic district and built in 1897, the Penny Farthing Inn is a Victorian-era home with eight eclectic rooms.

History

Penny Farthing Inn Bed and Breakfast in St. Augustine, FL was built in the early 1890's by Conrad Decker. Mr. Decker was a wealthy German who immigrated to Boston. He and his wife, Sophie, came to St. Augustine for the social seasons (January through March). He built the first Bridge of Lions for his train line to service the beach area. The inn fell upon hard times at several stages of its life. It was painstakingly restored between 1996 and 2001 by the current innkeepers—we have the scars to prove it! The work was chronicled on Home and Garden Television and the inn is now a shining example of Florida's Victorian architecture and a bygone era of dazzling wealth and privilege.

The Penny Farthing Inn Bed and Breakfast in St. Augustine

FL, may be over 110 years old but she is young by St. Augustine standards! In 1513, when Ponce de León first saw Florida, near the mouth of the St. Johns River, the flowers were in full Easter bloom so he called it La Florida (the flowering). Although de León did not stay long, the name has never left us.

In 1562, a French Huguenot settlement at the mouth of the St. Johns River was considered to be a serious enough threat by Philip II of Spain for him to send an expedition to rout it. That expedition, led by Pedro Menéndez de Avilés, succeeded and then moved down the coast. Menéndez left a small force in the natural harbor of "St. Augustín." On that site, on September 8, 1565, Menéndez officially claimed Florida in the name of Spain. The native Timucuans looked on in disbelief.

St. Augustine continued as the center of Spanish control for the Atlantic coast. In 1586, the English sailor Sir Francis Drake attacked and burned St. Augustine but the Spanish rebuilt it. During the 16th, 17th and 18th centuries, St. Augustine suffered repeated attacks from English expeditions and from Native Americans but the Spanish managed to maintain control. However, under the Treaty of Paris, England acquired Florida as one of the prizes of the French and Indian War.

In 1783, England returned Florida to Spain but the United States succeeded in negotiating for full control of the peninsula and it became a territory of the young nation in 1821.

In 1845, Florida became part of the United States but in 1861 seceded from the Union and became part of the Confederacy. In 1862, St. Augustine surrendered to the Union forces and was occupied peacefully for the balance of the Civil War.

The end of the war marked the beginning of St. Augustine as a place to visit. Its Spanish-styled architecture, its outstanding natural surroundings and its perfect climate made St. Augustine a favorite of northern visitors.

Henry M. Flagler saw the city's enormous potential and purchased a railroad to bring passengers from New York to St. Augustine. The ride took less than 24 hours. His two grand hotels, the Ponce de León Hotel and the Alcazar, were grand enough to attract the rich and famous. St. Augustine was definitely on the map!

Ghost Stories

The house is one-hundred-twenty years old. We were visited by a medium in August this year and she stayed in the Cherry Rose room, on the second floor in the main house.

The next day at breakfast she said she had used an EVP recording device and had she heard a small girl, about three or four years, named Carrie.

She lay on the bed with the woman and told her she had drowned and was she her mummy. She had light-colored hair that hung down around her chin, slight wave but not curly. She also wore a floppy hat tied around her small chin with a ribbon. She had on a sailor blouse with a big bow hanging around her neckline in the front of blouse. She was a beautiful child!

The medium looked up the records and found out Henry Flagler's son had a daughter who was named Carrie that had died at the same age as the little girl she had seen.

*****

She said there was a man named Victor, a doctor, who gets mad when people sleep in the Cherry Rose or the Victoria Room. She sat outside and a lady came through the door at the side of the house and said, "Do you like my house?"

The medium replied, "Yes, it's very nice. Thank you for letting me stay here."

She and her guest stayed up all night and listened to see if anything else would happen. They stayed three nights, taking turns staying awake. All they heard were footsteps and voices in the attic.

*****

Other guests have seen objects being moved.

*****

In the attic we have toy soldiers and guests have said that they count them, and then the next day they are moved.

*****

Doors open and shut when guests are out. A voice is heard calling for guests to get up when they have an afternoon nap.

*****

There are lots of orbs around house. The medium said she thought there was residual energy and ghost activity.

Chapter 13
Chapman Inn

2 Church Street

PO Box 1067

Bethel, Maine 04217

207-824-2657 877-359-1498 FAX: 207-824-7152

Website: http://www.chapmaninn.com/

History

The building itself has a fascinating history, and indeed is featured in the photograph on the cover of "The illustrated History of Bethel." It is one of the oldest structures in Bethel, having been built in 1865 by a retired sea captain.

The house attained a place in history when William Rogers Chapman purchased the home shortly after its construction. Mr. Chapman was a famous 19th century composer, conductor, and founder of the Rubenstein Club and Metropolitan Musical Society, as well as the Maine Music Festival. It is because of Mr. Chapman that Bethel could boast of its very own opera house, which to this day still stands, facing the Chapman House.

The Chapman House remained in the Chapman family until the 1950s. Unlike many New England buildings, the home has not been subjected to periodic additions.

Ghost Stories

The Chapman Inn is the only officially "certified haunted" inn in western Maine. After many years of strange happenings here at the inn, a certified paranormal investigator was called upon to do an in depth study.

*****

Some of the many unexplained events include doors that open and close by themselves, footsteps where no one is there, and cold drafts in closed rooms...even during the summer.

*****

Female voices, one very young, have been heard coming from empty rooms.

*****

There have been two reported sightings of a black cat that exited the room quickly when the room was entered. Normally this would not be an issue, except the cat left the room through a solid wall!

*****

Our paranormal investigator spent several days on this investigation, utilizing all of the modern and accepted techniques, including electronic detection and monitoring.

His summation indicated that the inn is definitely haunted, and almost certainly by at least two entities. He feels certain that one of the spirits is very likely that of Abigail Chapman. She was the invalid daughter of William Rogers Chapman, an early and long-time owner of the home.

Abigail Chapman was not a healthy child, and indeed was so precarious that William Chapman brought into the home a companion/nanny for her. Throughout Abigail's short life (she died at the age of 16) her companion was her only friend and social outlet.

After Abigail passed away, the companion stayed on in the

house, although in a somewhat different capacity. . When William Chapman died in 1927, he left a widow and several children, as well as a substantial fortune. However the home, along with enough money to operate it, he left in trust, (for as long as she lived or chose to live here,) to the companion.

Rumor has it that she had, at some point become, William Chapman's mistress. While the widow went to New York and enjoyed the life of a socialite, the companion stayed in Bethel and lived in this house until the day she died, in 1957.

The investigator theorized, with good evidence that even after death, Abigail would not leave her only friend and stayed on in spirit to be close to her. The investigator went on to state that there is very compelling evidence to indicate that there are two spirits who inhabit the inn. It is his professional opinion that the other spirit is that of the companion, who has also chosen to remain on this side, and that they will spend eternity forever united.

Over the years, it has become apparent that certain people are more sensitive to the unexplained events here at the inn than others. Though some will scoff at the thought of ghosts, we can testify that "something" inhabits the inn, and we leave it to the individual guest to decide for themselves what it is.

Pre-investigation
Interview with the Innkeepers Fred and Sandra

Para Patrol arrived at the inn at 1:00 PM and interviewed the innkeepers.

We learned that the most paranormal activity occurs in Rooms #4, #3, # 8 and # 9.

Guests have sighted a black cat in Rooms #7 and #9.

Some guests see the cat leave the room and disappear through the wall and other guests simply let the cat outside and later inform the innkeepers, "Your black cat was in our room and we let it outside." Of course, the innkeepers do not own a black cat.

Another guest reported seeing a young woman wearing a white nightgown in her room during the middle of the night. The guest said to the woman: "You are in the wrong room." The woman placed her finger to her lips and said, "Shhhh" and then vanished into thin air.

Housekeepers have heard young female voices in Rooms #7 and #9.

Perfume bottles have been reported to move from one room to another.

Footsteps are heard where there is no one and rocking chairs rock on their own.

Setup of Equipment and Preliminary Evaluation

We performed baseline temperature and EMF reading in Rooms #4, #7, #8, and #9.

We noted on our floor plans where EMF readings were obtained due to the presence of electrical equipment.

Preliminary EMF and temperature readings were routine except in Room #9 where we encountered an EMF reading on our Trifield meter of six milligauss where just minutes before the reading was zero. The EMF spike stayed steady at six in an area of approximately five square feet, notably just over the bed and on either side of the bed. Because this was an unexpected spike that stayed constant, we suspected that the Trifield meter was malfunctioning so we left the room with meter and the needle dropped to zero. Upon re-entering Room #9, the needle spiked back up to 6 milligauss and stayed constant for approximately thirty seconds and then dropped to zero. Photos were taken during this time and EVP session was immediately performed in Room #9.

Rooms #7, #8 and #9 are all in the same wing. There are no

other rooms in that wing.

Room #4 is in a different wing of the Inn.

IR cameras were positioned in Rooms #7, #8, and #9. Another was placed looking down the stairway from Rooms #7, #8 and #9.

A game camera, used for hunting, was positioned in Room #4 facing the rocking chair.

Due to the high EMF reading in Room #9, we ran a video camera positioned on the trifield meter and a K2 meter while we went out for dinner. We also placed the ping pong ball on the carpeted floor in Room #9.

A small perfume bottle was placed on the bureau in Room #7.

Investigation

Room #7: Kevin placed a ping-pong ball on the carpeted floor behind the chair near the foot of the right-hand side bed. Jayne started the video camera to record. Kevin noticed the ping-pong ball was gone. Jayne and Kevin searched the area but could not find it. Jayne was going to radio the other team when the walkie-talkie would not work and at the same time the video camera which was set on "record" went to "standby".

Room #9: No unusual activity observed during the investigation. We did not obtain abnormal EMF reading during the investigation in Room 9. EVPs were captured.

Room #8: No unusual activity observed during the investigation. EVPs were captured.

Analysis

We took 568 digital still photos, approximately 4 hours of video, 4 hours of IR video and 4 hours of audio. The video, digital still photos and game camera were all negative for paranormal anomalies.

EVP was captured in Rooms #7, #8 and #9.

Chapter 14
Charlemont Inn

Route 2, Mohawk Trail
Charlemont, MA. 0339
413-339-5796
charlotte.r.dewey@gmail.com

History

Built in 1787, The Charlemont Inn has served Mohawk Trail travelers for over 215 years. In this historic tradition, we offer reasonable and attractive guest rooms to suit the needs of all types of travelers. Guests of The Inn can be assured of a gracious welcome and a good night's sleep—but that is only the beginning

Our guest rooms have been nicely refurbished with antiques and period furniture for your comfort and enjoyment. Nothing about the ambiance is contrived—the charm is all natural and we look forward to sharing it with you. The amenities provided for our guests include specialty room service and wonderful culinary offerings. Your hosts will make sure that your visit is an experience you'll warmly remember. The Charlemont Inn has been described as one of the most eclectic country inns in America.

The Mohawk Trail is defined by The Berkshires, a range of steep wooded hills set amidst a rolling landscape of great beauty conducive to year-round activity. If you love the outdoors, the area provides white water rafting and boating, mountain biking, hiking, hunting and fishing. During summer, the area hosts many cultural festivals, the music festival at Tanglewood, and the Mohawk Trail Concert Series in Charlemont. Ski resorts attract visitors in the winter, and the autumn foliage in The Berkshires is regarded as the most colorful in New England.

Ghost Stories
Given by Charlotte Dewey

At the bar, when we have a physic occasionally pass through, they tell me that I have thirty-five or forty people standing at the bar…but they're not paying me!

*****

We have been told we have seventy-six energy sources. We asked ourselves, "Do we leave or do we stay?"

It sounds awfully crowded at the inn. They say, "Well it's only normal that you get that many spirits that want to come to a place where there's lots of people and lots of activity. This is a common gathering place for people, whether it was townspeople or someone passing by on the trail.

There have been accidents all along this highway, old and new, because it has its little dangerous spots. People would they tell us that we sit on a couple of intersecting vortexes, so not only do we have our resident guests, but we have those that come and go through the vortex.

*****

A few years ago, we had a back door that used to always open up at 4:00 PM. The seat at the end of the bar would turn and nobody knew exactly who it was in it. We were talking one day and someone was commenting about the chair.

They said, "Well, you remember that innkeeper that used to come in and always sit in that chair?"

He'd passed away about twenty some odd years before and his wife had gone away for a long time. She finally came back to this area, and then also passed. Now that door doesn't open anymore and the chair doesn't turn. So I think that they've gone on to a higher place.

*****

For a long time in the mid 1800s, this inn was used as a gathering spot for the doctor to serve all the little towns around. Some of the mediums have seen patients here in one portion of the inn, on a regular basis.

*****

Our most famous resident spirit, I believe at this time, has gone on to a better place. Her name was Elizabeth, but it turned out that her name was actually Vidalia Elvira and she was fourteen years old. That was some time during the late 1930s. She was here to see the doctor, died of consumption and she inhabits Room #23

*****

We don't have any nasty ghosts; we have some that are a little mischievous. They really like hairdryers and eyeglasses. These jump between rooms on occasion. We find them at the completely opposite end of the inn, and we know it's not the staff.

*****

Oftentimes, in one part of the inn, people have seen a person in Revolutionary War garment. This used to be the barn, but now it's part of the inn. He seems to be hanging around at that end of the barn. We don't have all the history on him, but he comes and goes.

94

*****

In the newer side, not only are there old ghosts, but there are new ghosts as well. People sometimes forget, but the recent passing of local people and friends are going to end up here.

*****

We have a cook that passed away about fourteen or fifteen years ago, although he hadn't worked here in some time. His tobacco had a very distinctive smell. We would always smell that tobacco. It would start about 7:00 AM or 9:00 AM because that was the time he used to come in to work. The other cook, at that time, also knew him; not from working here but from being around town. She'd come, get me, and say, "Charlotte, such and such is here."

I'd come in and smell it too and we'd both say good morning then go about our day.

*****

We have someone, maybe Elizabeth, in Room #23. A couple of years ago, we had an older couple come to visit. Their vehicle was making a horrible sound. They were sure their engine was about to blow any second. They were directed here and then get to the garage down the street the next morning.

We were having a cabaret (musical show where we tell ghost stories and accounts of the inn.) We were trying not to pin-point the rooms because sometimes people don't like the fact that there is somebody else in the room with them. We try to pick out the people before we give them the room numbers that might have the most activity.

It was later into the evening and most everybody had gone upstairs when I was on my way upstairs and heard a car alarm go off. I thought, "What the heck?"

I looked out the window and went down to see what the ruckus was. The car sounded awful! When I got to the front door, it stopped. So, I was going back upstairs, got to the second floor and it went off again.

It happened three times and I thought about knocking on the couples' door. I knew that there must be something paranormal going on.

The next morning the gentleman came downstairs early. I asked him if he had heard his car alarm during the night. He said, "I know. We had the remote control over on the table and it woke us both up three times."

I said, "Yes I know, I went downstairs."

"It's never happened before. The alarm was just going off and that second time we moved it on top of the chest of drawers instead of the table. When it went off the second time it was moved back over to the table."

He said, "Maybe it had something to do with that story you were telling us last night at the cabaret.

I said, "Well yes, probably…it is Room #23.

*****

Now that the word was out that we do have some paranormal experiences, we've had many paranormal groups come with all of their fancy equipment. We also have lots of mediums and physics come as well.

*****

We know that we have a couple of small children that hang out on the stairs constantly. They're usually seen sitting on the stairs with a cat. There are a couple of spots in the inn where cats show up; people have seen and heard them.

*****

On the more moderate side of things, we had a tour bus here while the cabaret was going… that's what they came for. We were telling ghost stories and when the guests went out to the bus, they couldn't get in. The bus driver said that had never happened, in fact she had never locked the door of the bus in all the years she had been driving for that company…ever.

Everyone was convinced at that time. It took about twenty minutes of the driver, guests, staff, and me trying to get the door open. All of the guests were figuring out who would be with whom in what room. They had it all figured out and we gave up.

We were going to call somebody out to help. As we were standing with our backs turned towards the bus, and the door popped open. That made a lot of believers real quick!

*****

We employee a lot of young people; first jobs, etc. I've been here twenty years. Some of them would ask me if there are really ghosts in the building.

I would say, "I'm not going to tell you whether there is or there isn't. I'll just tell you some facts and you can decide for yourself." I'm not making these stories up. I might not have totally believed all of this before I came here, but now I don't have any doubts, nobody has to convince me."

We have a big slicer, an old one, but it works beautifully. It has a double on and off switch and both things have to happen to start it up. On several different occasions, and two different times during the middle of that ghost story, that slicer turned on. We were not anywhere close to it and I had no trick buttons. That made some real quick believers out of those young people!

*****

The spirits are lost in a different plain and bump into things. Sometimes they see those modern things and it confuses them.

*****

We've had some interesting images. About seventeen or eighteen years ago, they would actually show up in the pictures. Now, people come with their digital cameras and orbs and faces will show up all over the place.

We never had any bad ones, just mischievous. Most of those might have been Elizabeth and a couple of other ones; we never had their names. They are mostly peaceful. Many people that come feel that they add to the energy of the building in a good way, not in a bad way.

*****

When I go in the basement, I'm always saying, "Hello. Is anybody down here?" (It's better to be safe than sorry.)

*****

We often hear slamming doors, especially through the center hall upstairs. This is the oldest part of the inn. That's probably where there have been some changes over the course of time. We are not privy to what it looked like back in the early days.

*****

Sometimes, paranormal groups come with their fancy technology. They stay in one room hoping to catch them. The room that they stayed in had no activity. They don't set it up in the room where everything is going on; they want to move it and the activity does switch.

If the spirits don't like the group, we have nothing but power surges and little mischievous things going on in the building for several days after they've left. This has happened two different times, and I know that they are telling me that they didn't like that group particularly, and not to bring them back!

Chapter 15
Chestnut Hall B & B

104 Lincoln Way West
New Oxford, PA 17350
1-888-886-5660
chestnuthallbb@yahoo.com
Website: http://www.chestnuthallbb.com/photos.html

History

This old house has quite a history. In March of 1888, Alexander W. (born 1854) and Sarah E. Himes (born 1857) purchased the property from McClelland and John Hersh. Now the Himes family was rich in history and prominence. Alexander W. Himes was the son of Thomas and Susan C. Himes who moved from Lancaster County to the New Oxford area when Alexander was a mere boy. Sarah E. whose parents were William and Mitilda Reed of York County married Alexander on March 1, 1885.

When they bought lot #82 in 1888, they commissioned the prominent architect John A. Dempwolf of York, PA to design and build what is now the very said property of 104 Lincoln Way West, New Oxford. They immediately began construction on a house that took them until 1890 to complete. Many changes were made from the original blueprint designs during the construction of the house. Some of the notable features original to the house are the beautiful set of stained glass windows in the staircase and the chestnut woodwork, which is abundant. The library bookshelves are a grand example of this artisanship.

Alexander had a very illustrious career in the shoe manufacturing business and later as a Director of the First National Bank of Hanover. He died at the young age of 53, on November 25, 1907, when he contracted typhoid fever and died in the very same house he had built. The house was then bequeathed to his wife.

Sarah E. Himes was also a well-known and respected citizen of New Oxford. It was said that during her care a two-story addition was built onto the house consisting of a kitchen and servant's quarters. Additionally, she refaced the existing fireplace in the living room, which of course gives a more massive and masculine look to the room. On April 17, 1931, Sarah died of "complications"; also in this very house.

Their surviving daughter Ruth Reed Himes inherited the family fortune, which included this property. She was born in this house the same year the house was completed (1890). Ruth grew up and met Hubert B. Flaherty (also known as Timothy) and they married on September 27, 1923. She was an avid gardener and a member of the Garden Club of New Oxford. Some landscape design features are still evident in the wonderful gardens that show themselves during the spring and summer.

Hubert became an officer of the Farmers and Merchants Bank of New Oxford. Ruth died on Dec 9, 1968 at the age of 78. She spent her entire childhood and adult life to the care and nurturing of this spectacular house. Hubert passed away on January 10, 1971, just a few years after Ruth's passing. Alexander W. and

Sarah E. Himes and Hubert B. and Ruth R. Flaherty are all buried in the New Oxford Cemetery.

Since the late 1970's the house has had four other owners that tended and cared for the history and reverence of this grand old lady. The current owners, Tina and Steve McNaughton have recently redesigned and renovated the kitchen to depict some old character qualities with modern amenities. With other renovations and changes completed Tina and Steve opened "Chestnut Hall Bed and Breakfast" for business in the spring of 2004. This old house exudes the grand Victorian splendor of yesteryear with the comforts of home.

We wish to extend our highest gratitude to The Adams County Historical Society in Gettysburg Pennsylvania. They were very instrumental in researching and obtaining the facts, names and dates that make up the saga of what is now Chestnut Hall Bed and Breakfast. And due to their information we were able to find and become great friends with the son of Tim (Hubert) and Ruth; Bill Flaherty and his wife Mim. It is due to their personal accounts and history that we are able to document all that we know of their family.

Paranormal Happenings

Allen Gross, a paranormal investigator and spirit photographer from Roanoke Virginia came to New Oxford for a weekend visit and investigation. Allen stayed with me (Steve McNaughton) at my bed and breakfast (Chestnut Hall). In addition to visiting several sites in the Gettysburg Battlefields, we also took a walk around the northwest end of New Oxford, which included around Chestnut Hall Bed and Breakfast. Lincoln Way West (Route 30) has several properties that have documented spirit hauntings including Chestnut Hall Bed and Breakfast. During this investigation, a few photos revealed some of the spirits in New Oxford. Allen also had a firsthand mischievous encounter.

Investigation Details

Allen arrived at Chestnut Hall on Friday late afternoon. Around 9:30 PM, the two of us got together for a walk around the northwest section of town. New Oxford is a small town so the walk did not take long.

Our first stop was in the rear garden at Chestnut Hall where we took a few photos, thermal readings, and video recording using infrared. After spending perhaps ten minutes in the garden, we moved to the front of the property and headed-west on the brick sidewalks on Lincoln Way West. We traveled about three blocks and turned north for one block and turned east onto Golden Lane which ran between Golden Lane Antiques and the local funeral home returning to Chestnut Hall where Allen stayed for the next two nights.

The general weather for the evening was clear, no wind with a temperature of 80 degrees Fahrenheit.

Video Recordings

The videotaping during this investigation was limited to the gardens at Chestnut Hall. Only five minutes into the taping, Allen and I stopped by a statue that was placed in memory of the lady who built the house and established the gardens. As I stated this aloud, I also asked if she could give me any sign that she was there. At that moment, Allen took this photo capturing an orb. In the viewfinder of the camcorder, I could see the flash from Allen's camera as well as all the moths and bugs flying around as they were picked up with the infrared lighting.

Upon review of the tape, we discovered something else was recorded. I actually captured a pair of orbs that illuminated with the camera flash, one of which is visible on Allen's photo. Based on our positions in the yard, I believe the second orb would have been behind the statue in the photograph. This three-second clip from the video is untouched or enhanced. The orbs are illuminated only as long as the camera flash, only one frame of the video.

Thermal Readings

We also had several instances of temperature drops. One of these fluctuations occurred immediately after we captured the orbs by the statue in the garden. At that time, the temperature dropped from 80 degrees to 67 degrees. A second temperature drop occurred in front of the B&B on the sidewalk as Allen took the photo with the ecto hand on my shoulder.

A thermal reading was not recorded at that time but the reason Allen took the photo was because I noticed and mentioned that I felt a very cold air encompass me. The third temperature fluctuation occurred while we were standing at the intersection of Golden Lane and Water Street. I was giving Allen a bit of history about the old shoe factory there and stories of the building when again I felt the temperature drop. Allen watched the readings on the thermal detector drop from 78 degrees to 31 degrees and then climbs back up to normal. There was no breeze or cold front blowing through New Oxford in the middle of that summer night.

General Thoughts

This is Allen's recollection and documentation of his stay at Chestnut Hall Bed and Breakfast on July 6 and 7, 2007.

After staying the first night and sleeping like a baby, I found no orbs, or ectoplasm and I took 187 pictures of the inside of the house. There were no feelings of being watched, no coldness, nothing heavy on or around my chest or shortness of breath. Just Comfort!

Night number 2. Climbing the stairs was breath taking. I had a feeling of being watched while changing the tapes in the camcorder in the Mahogany Suite. 12:13 AM, in my room while reviewing the pictures, a cold chill was felt. My back was to the hallway. 3:05 AM.; waking up, then feeling a sharp punch to the bed (when something is present, you'll wake up because of the different atmosphere.) I was awake for 10 seconds before the bump. Lying back down, I waited.

Twenty minutes later another bump on the right side of the bed. It felt like someone was taking their fist and hitting the bed as hard as they could. Getting out of bed, (I thought at first that this was Steve playing tricks.) Then I heard the doorknob rattle.

Going into the hall towards the bathroom, I heard a tap in the area of the door. Opening the door, I went into the hall; again there was a tap on the wall in front of me. I stepped on the hall step and heard my door slowly SHUT. We talked about this door earlier. It doesn't shut by itself and will not stay shut without help. I had no problem opening the door to go back inside the room.

Going outside on the balcony, I kept getting the feeling of being watched. Around 3:30 AM all bad feelings stopped, no more being watched. Nothing occurred the rest of the night. I went back to sleep after getting my camera and preparing myself for anything. I stayed awake until approximately 4:30, just waiting for a picture.

After the first night I would have gone home, not believing Chestnut Hall was haunted. After the second night, I can now say that Chestnut Hall is very haunted. I'm not a psychic, but I know when I'm cold and my hearing is perfect, this was no dream or imagination. I like Steve, look for facts and then try to figure out the reality of the situation.

You (Steve) asked about the two little kid spirits in the house. I never took a picture with you or your wife inside the house that weekend. All orbs were outside the house. I went through two tapes on the camcorder in the Mahogany Suite. The first tape ran when you and your wife were at the battlefield on Friday night.

Nothing happened until the two of you went to bed. The second tape is full of electrical interference. Kids will be kids. They follow you and your wife around. When I take pictures of either of you, I get orbs and ectoplasm. If you are not in the room, there is nothing. Wherever you go, they follow.

Chapter 16
Muriel's Jackson Square

801 Chartres Street
New Orleans, LA. 70116
504-568-1885 Fax: 504-568-9795
info@muriels.com
Website: http://www.muriels.com/html/home.html

History

1718—The year New Orleans was founded, a young French Canadian named Claude Trepagnier was a member of the expedition party led by Bienville that carved a clearing on the bank of the river and named it Ville de la Nouvelle Orleans. As a reward for his participation in the expedition, Claude Trepagnier was granted a plot of land where he constructed a house of brick between posts covered with ship-lap siding, a bark shingled roof, a brick chimney and a front gallery.

1721—The official design of the city was laid out.

The grid patterns of the streets of the new town were laid out with the center being the Place de Armes (parade grounds) which is now Jackson Square. The central focus of the traditionally designed French town was the Cathedral. With the laying out of the new city, Claude Trepagnier's house became a key plot of land.

Sometime Between 1743 and 1762

Jean Baptiste Destrehan acquired the property. He was the Royal Treasurer of French Louisiana Colonies and was a man of great wealth and power in New Orleans. He tore down the humble cottage and built a suitably fine home for his family. His residence was second only to the French Colonial Governor's Mansion which stood where the Presbytre is today. Jean Baptiste Destrehan outfitted and furnished the house with the best linens, fabrics, drapes, rugs, furniture, china, crystal and silver all of which was imported from Paris. The house is described in documents as having a drawing room, a music room, a ballroom, a dining room, 5 bedrooms, 3 cabinets, and a coach house with a kitchen.

1776—After the death of Jean Baptiste Destrehan in 1765 the house passed to his son and was then sold at auction when the family money ran out. In 1776 Pierre Phillipe de Marigny purchased the grand residence. Pierre Phillipe de Marigny used the house as one of his "city homes" when he came into town from his plantation on the outskirts of the town (now the Fauberg Marigny).

Ghost Stories
Ghosts, according to legend, are spirits who have not crossed over yet.

Ghosts, according to legend, are spirits who have not crossed over yet. Here at Muriel's, we are lucky enough to have a resident ghost, Mr. Pierre Antoine Lepardi Jourdan. Our Séance Lounges on the second floor are named as such because it is believed that this is where Mr. Jourdan spends the majority of his time.

*****

107

In 1788, there was a disastrous fire in New Orleans that burned 80% of the buildings in the French Quarter, including the original building on Muriel's property. The next year, Mr. Jourdan bought the property and built his dream home for himself and his family. He was, unfortunately, quite a heavy gambler, and one night in 1814 he wagered his beloved home in a poker game and lost.

Before he had to vacate, however, Mr. Jourdan committed suicide on the second floor, in the area where our Séance Lounges are situated today. Thus, Pierre Antoine Lepardi Jourdan never had to really leave his home, and continues to reside there to this day.

We also have a slightly mischievous ghost in our Courtyard Bar...one possibility is that Mr. Jourdan gets angry and goes downstairs to throw glasses to release some angst. Another possibility is that Muriel's has a second, slightly mischievous ghost that roams the property. Three times since March of 2001, glasses have flown from behind the bar twelve feet across to the brick wall and shattered.

*****

Muriel's also has a carriageway that dates back to the late 1700's, and some clairvoyants say that many troubled spirits reside here, for this area was said to be where servants were housed at night.

Our resident ghosts here at Muriel's are harmless, and can sometimes be very entertaining. So be on the lookout during your next visit to Muriel's...you might just experience more than our cuisine!

*****

Our waiter told us he was once having an argument with a co-worker he was dating, turned and his back was hit by flying sauce container. I turned to tell her she didn't have to hit me with anything only to discover she was on the other side of the room. Arguments seem to bring out the ghosts.

*****

In a draped corner, at the foot of the wooden staircase that leads to the Séance Lounge, a table had been set in tribute especially for Jourdan, replete with filled wine glasses and bread. As I climbed the staircase alone I felt as if someone was climbing behind me, always just one step below me. A half-hour later, I felt some sense of validation when I saw Taylor running quickly up the same otherwise empty staircase, slightly panicked, "Someone was watching you from behind on the staircase!" she cried.

After twenty seemingly uneventful minutes, we moved to the monitoring station, replaced by Gullette and Adams. Again, we asked Jourdan to give us a sign of his presence.

After absolute silence, a loud tap suddenly resounded on the table next to us. Duplechien, believing it was condensation dripping from the air conditioning vent overhead, checked the table to find it bone dry.

Something fell from me and dropped to the floor with a tinny sound. Adams and Gullette caught up with me on the staircase a little later and Adams handed me one of my earrings that she found on the floor of the Séance Room. My hands flew to my ears—both formerly very secured earrings were gone. Duplechein tells me the tinny sound we heard was the other earring falling when we were at the monitoring station invoking Jourdan to give us a sign of his presence.

"Amanda and I heard knocking noises going across the ceiling in the séance room two different times," said Adams, "but I found your earring. We felt footsteps, heard other random knocking noises in the room and both saw a black shadow type figure cross the room rather quickly."

*****

I got paired with Steve outside the suicide room. Randomly, I shot pictures aimed at the darkness with a digital camera. One of these catches the mirror outside the Séance Lounge. In the photograph, the word "CARD" appears in luminous writing across the face of the mirror.

*****

At the ghost's table, Duplechien was paired with Annie. "We were sitting at the table set for the resident ghost," said Annie, "and I felt my left pant leg tugged twice ... we went up to the séance room. Brandon and Rebecca where already there doing some EVP work."

After 2:00 AM, I left Coleman to join Thomas, Foltz, Taylor and Duplechien in the Séance Room. We were all sitting in the inner portion of the room and I was nearest the drapery dividers, looped back, hanging by evenly spaced curtain tabs. On the other side of the drapes, the outer portion of the lounge is deserted.

Thomas and Foltz had staged a mock argument and report that in response to their questions, they heard knocking sounds. One tap meant "yes," two meant "no."

I asked Jourdan why he went to the slave quarters to kill himself—a question that caused a barrage of insulting accusations to erupt from the rest of the team.

Provoking a spirit has been known to elicit responses, but Jourdan remained quiet to all insults. Thomas was very humorous with his questions, so I asked Jourdan if he liked this brand of humor. I immediately witnessed a white flash of light in a far corner, a sighting that was later substantiated by Foltz.

"When you said you saw a light in the upper corner of the room I also saw that same light out of the corner of my eye," she said.

Then, the tapping began; one quiet tap that occurred after each question is asked. It came from the empty outer room nearest to me. My skin crawled as a tap intelligently answered each question—I felt someone unseen near me. Duplechien sat directly across from the drapery dividers.

"The most interesting phenomena I personally encountered," said Duplechein, "was when I saw the shadowed object pass in front of the curtain immediately after the knocks were heard."

"The tapping appeared to be the result of a spirit attempting to communicate with us because the taps were often heard in response to our questions," said Foltz. We were able to regain communication with the spirit evidenced by the knocking that you witnessed in addition to the light in the corner."

It was now nearly 3:00 AM. The tapping was interrupted when we were informed that our hosts were tired and wished to go home.

"In minutes we heard knocks," said Taylor, "and started to see shadows … I heard two very heavy footsteps. I stopped to see who would be walking so heavily down the stairs and there was no one!"

Experiences from the restaurant staff:

Jessica: "The minute guests began speaking French, a perfectly balanced wine glass mysteriously flipped completely off my serving tray," she recalls. "Simultaneously, the tray of another waitress was knocked from her hands as though someone had deliberately struck it."

Ian: "When I make my rounds before leaving," Turkmen claims, "I feel a presence accompanying me upstairs near the Séance Lounge." Turkmen adds that the presence seems to hold no menace but feels mystical, and is someone he rather likes. "One night, while making my rounds alone in the building, a candle holder fell over by itself," he calmly states.

Mary: "I started working at Muriel's a year-and-a-half ago and I was on the second floor in the wine room adjacent to the Séance

Lounge (site of Jourdan's suicide.) Only the manager and I were in the building at the time. When I walked past the Séance Lounge, I saw a hot and hazy figure of a man. He was wearing clothes from the 1700s, dressed in red and gold, with a long jabot."

Nicole: "They (Austrian guests began having a discussion in German regarding woodworking) expressed the desire to sign one of the antique guest books. Before they could sign the book, another book flew to the floor and opened at random to a certain passage. The passage, written in German, was all about woodworking!"

*****

On the wall near the windows, two tiny handprints etched in black mar the finish. We're told only the workmen who were painting the gold leaf had keys to the premises and when they left, they locked everything. Although no one had access to the building overnight, the next morning the workmen arrived, these tiny handprints were found on the wall.

In a photograph taken by LaSpirit's Investigator Jennifer Broussard, would reveal a bright blue orb floating in that same hallway. **And in conclusion...**

The subsequent scrutiny of video by LaSpirits team members caught no ghostly apparitions drifting through the restaurant. But, team members (including me) reported seeing shadowy shapes in the Séance Lounge when responsive taping occulted. Complete review of the audio revealed marked Electric Voice Phenomenons (EVPs).

When the investigation began, co-director Broussard stated, "Here we go." EVP recordings immediately picked up a male voice not belonging to any team members mimicking her exact words. As investigator-in-training Rodney Grudmeyer sat at the ghost's table in the stairwell, a female voice with a French, almost Creole, accent, not belonging to any of the team members can be heard saying, "Thank you."

When Adams and Gullette replaced Duplechien and myself in the Séance Room, audio clearly picks up two long male moans or sighs and a gasping sound—as though someone was trying to catch his breath. All of the tapping sounds in response to our questions in the Séance Room towards the end of the evening were clearly recorded.

*****

This is a snippet of a story I wrote about one of our employees and a famous actress....

Another one of the things David loves about Muriel's is the clientele. There is a really great mix of tourists and locals. *A movie star, named Virginia*, has come in a couple of times and she now asks for David to be her waiter. Once, when David was giving a tour of the building to *Virginia*, they both got a little spooked because they felt an unexplained presence. He said they all noticed at the same time that the hair stood up on the back of their necks.

Well, during this tour, Virginia took a picture of David. She later returned to show David the picture and there was a presence behind him in the picture. This served to solidify his belief that ghosts do exist and are likely in our building.

Phone interview with Denise

On New Year's Eve, some of my friends were here. We have a "ghost table" that we keep there. My friend, who has a happy life, sat down at the table and pretended she was toasting our ghost. Another friend sat down and pretended like she was kissing our ghost. We took pictures directly in concession and you can see on the second picture my friend that's divorced and going through a really hard time there's an orb in that picture right where the ghost chair is. Very strange and peculiar...apparent and odd.

*****

We had a big costume party on Halloween night and my friend took a lot of pictures and there's a lot of stuff...so many orbs.

113

Chapter 17
Brookdale Lodge Inn and Spa

P.O. Box 903
11570 Hwy 9, Brookdale, CA 95007
Tel (831) 338-1300 Fax (831) 338-1303
info@brookdaleinnandspa.com
Website: http://brookdaleinnandspa.com/contact.html

History
Set under massive redwoods in the Santa Cruz Mountains, you will find the world famous Brookdale Lodge.

The original lodge was built in 1890 by Judge J.H. Logan at the site of the Grover lumber mill. In the early 1920's, Dr. F.K. Camp built the beautiful dining room with the natural brook running through it. A feature in "Ripley's Believe It or Not" served to make the Brookdale Lodge world famous. Throughout the years, the Brookdale Lodge has hosted a number of notable guests: movie stars, music celebrities and a U.S. President.

In 1890 Santa Cruz Bank President & Superior Court Judge James (John) Harvey Logan purchased the property.

The U.S. Post Office made Brookdale an official name when it was established in 1902 with the stores and dance pavilion that would support his town. He kept an eight acre lot for the hotel and the rest sold like hotcakes.

In 1911 Logan, William T. Jeter and I.T. Bloom sold 1,200 acres of Brookdale land to John DuBois of Santa Cruz, who planned to subdivide for vacation homes. That same year William M. Aydelotte bought the hotel, cottages, store, warehouse, stables and corrals. All that remained of Logan's holdings was the Post Office and the electric light and water company, which he continued to upgrade.

After Dr. F.K. Camp purchased the site in 1922, the river jumped its banks and changed course, cutting a seventy-foot length of lapping river through the hotel grounds.

The lodge's atmosphere inspired three songwriters to write "My Brookdale Hideaway," "A Place Known as Brookdale," and "Beautiful Brookdale Lodge." Many years later, the famous Ink Spots played at the lodge.

Hollywood stars including Mae West, Marilyn Monroe, Joan Crawford, Shirley Temple Black (She had a summer home her), Tyrone Power, Rita Hayward, Hedy Lamarr, Henry Ford and Howard Hughes were regulars. Politicians such as President Herbert Hoover and Cordell Hull visited the lodge and were pampered like kings. Also, visited by Chris Fleming of the TV show 'Dead Famous 'when he was doing an investigation on Joan Crawford.

Shortly before his death in 1945, Dr. Camp sold the property to A. T. Cook and W. G. Smith.

In 1951 it was again sold to a consortium of San Francisco businessmen and then to Barney Marrow, who also owned the Brookdale Inn across the highway.

After a fire on October 24, 1956 one of three major fires in the area that year. The fire destroyed the Brook Room and Peter Pundt's Saloon. When Morrow rebuilt the Brook Room in 1957 with a Butler building, it included the addition of a grand dome once belonging to a church. He often referred to his lodge as a "Hansel and Gretel theme motel," that he transformed into a mock French Tudor and a "Santa's Village Swiss" design. (Famous in Scotts Valley)

In 1989, real estate investor Bill & Lee Gilbert purchased the lodge and surrounding eight acres, and refurbished forty-six motel rooms, two cabins, the Brook Room and the lounge, which are open for business.

More than 165 years after it's opening, the lodge continues to register guests. Despite the history of flooding and fires, the river still runs through the Brook Room as it has for more than half a century.

Ghost Stories
Phone interview with Nancy Ward

"Sarah" knows Nancy. They had an investigation one time and the investigator said, "Hey, Sarah, Nancy's here."

A voice promptly responded with, "Where's Nancy?"

We even have her voice on a recorded saying, "Nancy's here!"
*****

Nancy plays with toys with her. Bubbles game is just what it sounds like...blowing bubbles. We would say, "Sarah come on...hit one, blow on one, just anything you want to do." On recorder soon after it started, they heard, "Time to play!" Sarah died there.
*****

Two investigators, D. and B., were in Room #4 resting on the bed. This was during the remodeling time. B. felt something on the bed by his calf/ankle area that startled him. He looked and nothing was there.

D. put her hand on it and felt a very cold spot. They could see nothing, but they said it felt like a cat in between his calves, trying to make a bed to take a nap. This was at 5:00 PM.

After the investigation, they came up to rest and the same thing happened to D.

*****

The "Log Cabin Room" was the original entrance to the lodge. It was a speakeasy during prohibition era and alcohol, drugs, and woman were snuck in.

A nasty man entity shows up there. He even threw a part of a shingle at us by the wood shed one day.

We tried to find out his name. We feel as if he is from the prohibition period and has responded to both Vincent and Francis; so most likely is Italian.

If you provoke him, you may get called a few nasty names, like bitch, or worse and a "get out or go away" mixed in.

*****

Nancy had her recorder outside the log cabin one day, preparing to bring in a tour. She wanted to visit to get someone or something to respond.

She said, "I'm Nancy and I will be bringing a crowd with me so be prepared to talk or something with them.

As I was walking out the door, Mr. Logan said, "Bye" softly and nicely, "nice to meet you."

Mr. Logan was a judge that started the first water company, electric company and post office, which made Brookdale an actual city.

The lodge used to be where a lumber mill was. There were many shacks and a graveyard. A major fire burned everything down. Dr. Cook was Mormon. He built back the camp in the 1920s but allowed no smoking, drinking, etc. If he saw you with a glass, he would pick it up, smell it, and throw you off the property if any whisky.

*****

A fourteen-year-old child died in the pool in 1972. Now, many people see "sparks" in the pool area.

*****

During the prohibition era, they used have the Mermaid Room. Each mermaid would have a number on her and would swim in front of the glass window for the people to see. A man would choose a number, and the mermaid would climb out of the pool and be whisked away via an underground tunnel to the cabins where she would meet the gentleman.

Many celebrities have stayed here over the years. For example: Marilyn Monroe, the Kennedy's, Joan Crawford, famous gangsters, and more.

The tunnels have been caved in now because a road was built on top and they didn't want it to fall in.

*****

While cleaning up after the fire at Dr. Cook's camp, bodies were supposedly left between the indoor pool and a section of the rooms. It has been reported that we have forty-five to fifty spirits with us.

*****

You would think that around the brook would be hard to pick up with a voice recorder; just the opposite. It creates a white noise that makes it much easier for voices to come through loud and clear.

*****

Paranormal Activity: Lodge is now nicknamed 'Little Stanley'

Gilbert family—1989—daughter, Kim experienced doors slamming, Jukebox and television began to blare on their own. Toilet paper rolls unwound simultaneously from the men and women's restrooms. She would wake to someone calling her name at 3:00 AM. Then, hearing laughter from the conference room as well as sounds of someone playing pool and no one was there. They saw a little girl in old-fashioned clothing running through the lobby and then disappearing.

*****

James Harvey Logan—has been seen in the lobby sitting in a chair watching people come and go.

Sarah (6yrs old), was Mr. Logan's niece. She would go up to guests and ask have you seen my Mommy. They would get glimpse of her in the restaurant. You can hear her giggle, and speak to you with your own ears even though you can't see her. EVPs of her saying "look at me" "Hi, Nancy" and they actually heard with their own ears "Where's Nancy."

*****

Sarah's mother has been seen in the restaurant. We feel she is looking for Sarah.

*****

In the cabin room a shingle was thrown at an investigator. EVPs of gangster type of characters.

*****

Indoor pool area, 1972, a thirteen-year old girl drown.

*****

Caretakers and employees report they hear furniture moving while they are cleaning up.

This area would be locked up and the next day there would be furniture in the pool sitting perfectly up right.

*****

Music can be heard in some of the rooms, even though there's no band playing.

*****

Room #4 reports of feeling like a cat had jumped on the bed and getting comfortable

*****

Strange sensations in the garden section of the hotel are experienced. Reported, but not confirmed, that this is where the old cemetery was when the lumber town existed. They cleaned up the area but did not move the graves.

Energy is not destroyed, but a different form with different ways to communicate.

Chapter 18
Burn Brae Mansion

573 High RoadGlen Spey, NY
12737845-856-3335—Burn Brae
officeinfo@BurnBraeMansion.com
Website: http://burnbraemansion.com/contact.htm

History

Burn Brae Mansion was completed in 1908 by George Ross Mackenzie as a wedding gift to his daughter, Margaret Elkin.

Mackenzie, third president of the Singer Sewing Machine company, made his fortune as confidant and advisor to Isaac Merritt Singer, the company's founder. Rich in history, Burn Brae Mansion was recently restored for its 100-year anniversary.

Following the renovations, the original servants' quarters, now named the Singer Suite and Elkin Room, and the adjoining guest rooms, now named the Mackenzie Suite, were opened to the public. Shortly after reopening, overnight guests began reporting mysterious sights and sounds during their visit. Further research revealed a history of such reports, and subsequently spurred curiosity about the previous occupants of Burn Brae.

As part of the research, on August 18, 2007, a team of 14 ghost hunters spent the night documenting the activity in the Singer Suite. Their results are documented on the Paranormal Research page.

Paranormal Research
"Your creepy location scared the living daylights out of us!"
Jason and Grant
Ghosthunters, Sci-Fi Channel

On a beautiful night in August, Ghosthunters from SJGR arrived at the mansion complete with motion sensors, digital cameras, digital voice recorders, and infrared thermometers, as well as some sensory abilities of their own.

Their research uncovered evidence that was off the charts compared to an average investigation.

They found one hundred eighty-six positive photos two positive videos and five motion sensor readings, which were described as well above average. They also picked up forty-seven EVPs and thirty-two Positive Anomalous EMF readings, which is extremely high. Almost all of the sensory investigators reported an overwhelming sense of spirit activity accompanied by cold patches, pressure and emotional swings.

The following are some samples of the evidence:

Investigator Denise J.

10:48pm "During my EVP attempt I asked if there was anything that they would like us to know. I started receiving pressure in the front of my head and at the same time S. started to receive cold chills."

10:49pm "R. claims he hears a voice but it is not clear enough to discern what it is saying."

10:51pm "I started to feel pressure all over my body again."

10:52pm "I kept feeling compelled to ask 'is your baby ok?' and if something had happened to her child. I also wanted to keep looking for something but I wasn't sure exactly what it was I was looking for so I asked if there was something in particular she wanted me to find."

10:53pm "I heard a distant female voice saying 'No, no, no' in a grieving manner. It was almost like she was wailing. R. had also heard the same voice."

10:54pm "I then asked if the baby's name was 'Levi', at which time I got the chills and goose bumps. Sharon also claimed that the temperature felt as though it had dropped and it had gotten considerably cooler. I also got the impression that the baby had passed in the home and that the mother is still in the mansion grieving the loss of her son."

10:55pm "I then heard the same female voice crying out and sobbing. R.also heard this. So I asked if there is something here that she wanted us to find that reminded her of her baby. Immediately after that question S., R., and I heard the female voice let out a wail that sounded very distraught and grieved. We questioned everyone later if anyone had heard anything like we heard and no one heard a thing."

10:56pm "S., R. and I started feeling pressure on the left side of our heads. Again we noticed a very cold chill in the air at which time my radio started making a static noise. I was standing up and it was located in the lower pocket of my cargo pants so it was impossible to have accidentally hit any buttons."

Conclusion

"Based on my psychic impressions, the unexplained voices heard and the unexplained scientific evidence collected I do believe there to be many layers of spirit activity in the mansion. Although Nothing I experienced was harmful or malignant in anyway. I do believe there to be both intelligent and residual haunting present."

Investigator Maureen C.

9:59pm "An orb is seen moving on the left wall of the second floor hallway from bottom to top—captured on the Sony camcorder."

10:21pm "I find the batteries in my Kodak digital camera are completely drained of power."

10:23pm "The battery power has drained from the ELF Zone EMF detector."

11:24pm "I hear a man's whisper near me as I sit on the steps leading to the second floor."

3:11am "I start recording my audio when I reach the 3rd floor attic bedroom where I will be sleeping. As I was approaching the room I felt as if someone ran their fingers across the top of my head."

3:12am "A male voice is recorded on my Sony camcorder saying 'You need to go'".

3:16am "I set my Sony DVR on the night stand to record for the remainder of the night."

3:19am "I settle down to sleep."

3:46am "A female voice is recorded on the Sony DVR saying 'Sleep'"

3:51am "A male voice is recorded saying 'Good Night.'"

Conclusion

"There is no doubt in my mind that there are spirits inhabiting the Burn Brae Mansion. Despite the long hours of recording audio on both the digital voice recorder and the camcorder, I've found a very large amount of Electronic Voice Phenomena recorded during this investigation. I do not believe that any of these spirits are threatening or anything negative. Even the spirit on the second floor appears to be more cantankerous than anything else and if guests are ever frightened by spirit activity they should be aware of this fact."

Investigator David H.

9:58pm "I started to feel light headed on the porch."

2:06am "My digital recorder came on by itself."

3:57am "I saw a small child size shadow moving in the dining room."

Conclusion

"There were two impressions that stand out. The first was every time I went towards the big tree on the right side of the home I felt a heavy sensation and it felt as if someone was drawing me towards the tree to feel their sadness. The second was when investigator Ros was attempting an EVP in the first floor main room my eyes started to water and I felt sad. I felt there was a lot of spirit activity here."

Investigator Randy N.

10:30pm "Denise senses the name Joanne in the year 1913. I felt pressure building in the room at that point. Sharon and Denise sense a young woman with brown hair and chubby cheeks."

10:48pm "I keep getting the impression someone is standing near me."

Conclusion

"At many points within the mansion I felt a heaviness and found it hard to catch my breath. I felt as though someone was with me at some points and experienced sounds that were unexplainable.

Without a doubt there is something within the walls of this residence and on the property.

At no time did I feel threatened and I do not believe these entities are there to hurt anyone but to have a story to communicate."

Investigator Dave C.

10:40pm "I feel pressure in my head."

10:47pm "I feel tightness in my throat and dizziness."

2:38am "My radio activates for no known reason."

Conclusion

"I felt heaviness in the upstairs sitting room. I also had the feeling of a presence in the second floor hallway. In addition, I saw something small run

down the bottom of the landing of the large staircase and various noises were heard throughout the night. Considering the high rate of positive photo's and positive EVP's that were captured throughout the site, I would say that this location is definitely active."

Investigator Dawn A.

10:39pm "At the tree outside the right side of the house I felt like something was watching us."

11:25pm "I went up the first flight of stairs and felt a major pressure on my chest."

2:20am "I wanted to try the second floor again. While sitting in the sitting room I felt some chills and uneasy."

Conclusion

"While investigating the Burn Brae Mansion I got the impression that something was going on in the house. I believe that there is a lot of activity in the house. Even though I didn't get evidence on film or my digital recorder, what I felt was real."

Investigator Jessica B.

10:58pm "I started to feel a tingling on my right side of hair and neck."

11:05pm "I kept on getting this feeling of someone sitting on the chair next to the bed I was sitting on. Christine senses a woman in the chair next to me caressing my hair."

Conclusion

"I felt heaviness in my chest when we entered the sitting room on the second floor and also felt like someone was watching us from the hallway. In the second bedroom where I felt my hair tingling I got this thought that a women gave birth in the house or the room and that someone always sits by the side of the bed in the chair.

With the personal experience I can say that I feel that there is spirit activity and that there may be several spirits in different rooms. I also feel that with numerous positive readings from the cell sensor EMF detector that there is a lot of activity. I felt many different feelings, emotions, tension in each room that we investigated in. I did not feel threatened or afraid."

Investigator Marti H.

10:38pm "An investigator stated she had a feeling of cold over her left shoulder. A positive photo was taken at this time."

11:57pm "I saw something move by the front door. A positive photo was taken."

1:25am "EVP Attempted on a digital voice recorder...I had a very strong feeling of pressure on my chest and loss of breath."

4:30am "I heard footsteps and what sounded like furniture moving above the third floor."

Conclusion

I felt a heavy and anxious feeling from the time I walked into the building. The feeling got stronger on the 2nd floor in the sitting room and the attic.

I believe there to be a lot of spirit activity through the house. The stronger activity seems, for me, to be on the 2nd and 3rd floors. I did get feelings of activity on the first floor and on the grounds around the house as well."

Investigator Maureen C.

1:54am "I sensed a presence passing through the entryway just after a second team of investigators passed through the room and out the front door."

2:24am "The batteries in my radio and in investigator Clendaniel's flashlight and digital voice recorder suddenly died."

3:22am "I sensed a presence in the room and felt tightness in my chest."

3:39am "I heard a creak or a crackling sound coming from the dining room."

3:49am "I sensed an overwhelming presence in the room and began to feel shaky. I received a positive photo."

4:57am "I saw something move by the baby carriage. I obtained a positive photo."

Conclusion

"I felt a very strong presence in the 2nd floor sitting area while passing

through it during our preliminary walkthrough of the property but found it had dissipated when my team returned there to investigate hours later. The most active area psychically in my opinion was the entire first floor. There was a sense that spirits regularly roam that area. Some appeared to be aware of our presence and seemed to resent the intrusion very late into the investigation. The dining room seemed to have shadows moving through it.

I felt faint indications of spirit activities in all areas of the building. The first floor was extremely active. Overall I believe that there are several ghosts that are active in this location."

Investigator Kathleen S.

10:25pm "I was sitting in a chair by the door and smelled a strange odor." (Orb photos were taken)

10:42pm "A felt a male presence in the room." (Orb photos taken)

Conclusion

"The mansion is full of spirit activity all at different levels due to the number of families that have lived there. It was sometimes overwhelming. There are even spirits of cats there. It seemed that none of the spirits knew each other or were aware of other spirits. They definitely became tired of us and were indicating that we should leave them alone. Eventually they stopped communicating with us."

Investigator Eileen S.

11:34pm "While descending the servant stairway, I closed the door behind me on the landing. As I turned from it the door handle jiggled very hard as if someone was trying to open it. I obtained a positive EVP."

1:37am "I receive an impression of an old man pacing the hallway and the motion sensor alarm went off not long after. Both Investigator Dave C. and I picked up the same EVP on separate recorders at this time."

Conclusion

"Throughout the investigation I could feel the presence of spirits around

me, walking into the room, coming close to me but was not able to examine more closely who or what they were on this visit due to my monitoring of the teams. I could feel a woman in the second floor sitting room. The energy was very strong in there as it also was in the hallway that leads to it. There was a certain area of this hallway, near the small stairs that lead to the sitting room that felt like I hit a wall and could not walk further down the hallway. I felt that there was an older man who worked there at some point in this area and was not happy with us being there. He wore a white or light colored shirt and dark pants.

My body ached all night until we left the home, then the pain dissipated. I felt that I was experiencing sympathetic pain from someone with chronic pain or illness that once lived or worked there.

I feel the Burn Brae Mansion is very active with several spirits, all benign, some residual (like an echo in time) some interactive and conscious of us (grounded).'

Investigator Sharon C.

10:54pm "I feel extreme cold chills and notice that my radio was turned off. The batteries had died but had been at full power earlier."

1:31am "The motion sensor detects movement in the hallway. I take a positive photo."

1:39am "The motion sensor detects movement in the hallway again. Another positive photo taken."

Conclusion

"While investigating the grounds surrounding the house I got the impression of the large tree being used to hang someone. I was unsure if this was a suicide or murder. I also felt a male presence watching our team from the path, who would retreat when we approached but stayed close by to observe us.

There seemed to be many active areas in the mansion as well as on the grounds. While there did seem to be a female spirit who was distressed and searching for something, none of the spirits felt threatening or harmful."

Interview with Andy Russ

A couple of years ago, we ran haunted hayrides.

We were checking the trail one night and heard a pack of snarling, barking dogs.

I said, "My God, what is that? What should we do?"

"Start climbing the tree!" Alan (his brother) hollered back.

We started to climb and heard what sounded like the dogs coming out of the woods. They sounded like they were right on top of us! Suddenly all went quiet. We heard nothing, no walking off...nothing. Just *dead* silence.

We just looked at other like, what the ...?

*****

A year after that Mike Fraysse, the property owner, discovered a pet cemetery on the property where people buried their animals. There was a well out there also where animals had fallen into.

He accidentally dug up a dog within a few feet of where we heard the barking. There are as many haunted pets as humans on the grounds of Burn Brae.

When they came out of the woods they were very intuitive of what they heard.

*****

In my apartment above the inn, I thought someone was outside or in the basement making noise. I thought I heard a ghost; it sounded like the fake ghost sounds you usually hear of...booooo! Fake. I thought someone was playing a joke on me. Outside was pitch black, no wind. I didn't chalk it up to anything.

Later, when I went back into the apartment, my dog Katy wouldn't go in. I had to go get a leash and actually pull her in. She went in and jumped on the bed and sat straight up, staring into the kitchen. She did this all night...just sitting up at attention on the bed, looking into the kitchen. I didn't sleep that night.

*****

We have an animal ghost. We found a mummified cat in basement.

*****

There is a man on the steps by the bathroom.

*****

Interview with Art Petersen

Art is part of an acting troop at Burn Brae,—The Dark Forest. They set up interactive scenes in the woods for haunted attractions and Halloween shows.

The mansion was actually haunted for quite some time before the owners even realized it. Every night we would hang out there and put all of our outfits and masks away, then go up to the mansion for a nightcap.

The end of October 1994, which was the season's last day, we had a cast party in the main ballroom. If you open up the front main doors there is a huge room.

*****

There is a landing from the first floor and then you go up the main staircase. I was hanging out one time, during the night. Everyone was doing some dancing and drinking. I got tired, so I sat down on the landing at the bottom of the main staircase.

The lights were on in the main ballroom and I looked over at the glass on the closed front doors. I could clearly see myself sitting down and I saw a man standing right behind me. He had on turn-of-the-century clothing, a long trench coat or overcoat. He was medium height (5'8 or 5"9.) His hat was an old style, not quite western, shorter, and cropped with a brim. I looked and there was nobody behind me. I turned back and the man was still there in the reflection...I felt him

*****

I have ESP and am a clairvoyant...like a spirit portal. Lots of spirits try to communicate through me. I am not exactly a psychic, but I've had the ability to tell people certain things because of a very strong presence; in a nutshell, the things that I feel.

Lots of activity happens around me if I am in a haunted house or area. Ever since I was a kid, I've seen many ghosts, apparitions, and paranormal things.

It's something like if you were to come into a dark room, and you can feel somebody is staring at you. Then you turn on the light and there actually is someone there…you can feel their presence. It is the same with a spirit if their energy is just right, you can feel them.

*****

People back in the old days would go by the feeling they would have and could tell that there was somebody in the room. There are a lot of skeptics that wouldn't believe it; acknowledge it if you believe. I pick up on people who are there all the time.

*****

I met this man; turns out he is a "history buff" who lives in the neighborhood. He told me there was a guy who had actually fallen down the staircase and broke his neck; maybe he's been hanging around there ever since at the bottom or top of the stairs.

*****

On November 1, 2008 Andy was conducting a haunted tour of the mansion. He invited me to come up because he knows that if I'm around, the spirits will come out.

*****

We started in the main ballroom with me sitting right at the bottom of the stairs. I immediately felt someone standing behind me. They had asked me to be a part of this tour so I said, "If you guys want something to take home with you, get your digital cameras out and take a picture of me."

They did just that and every shot that I'm in; there is a spirit orb behind me. After I got up, you could see the orb cruising up the staircase.

Spirits show up as orbs in photos. Occasionally they'll show up as full-body apparitions, but it takes an awful lot of energy to manifest that. The lens of a camera is better than a lens of an eyeball. More precise...and it's not subject to interpretation. Many people don't know how to comprehend what they see. Some exaggerate, or think that orbs are dust spots on the lens. You must learn how to comprehend what you see.

If you were to see a dust spot on the lens, you would see an out of focus circle. A spirit orb has a very sharp, clean edge to it. You can see it; it is very distinct.

We went through the whole tour and people were taking pictures in various rooms with EMS meters going off, and then taking pictures, and they are able to see spirit orbs.

After Andy finished taking them through the mansion, (all three floors) he would lead everybody out through the back and walk down the "Haunted Trail" where we would put on the Halloween Show.

The trail goes through the woods for about twenty-eight acres. You then come to the backstreet that cuts through the woods and it's all dark and spooky. Across from the backstreet is the big graveyard.

Most interesting activity happens there. This was a night where it was still warm enough outside. It was probably mid to upper 40s, but not quite cold enough where you would see your breath at all in any of the pictures. We had no condensation. We are, after all, at the McKenzie part of the graveyard site. What you do see in pictures with me taken with Andy, guests, and my wife, are astral mists that appear on film and they will be forming faces in the mist.

All the hair went up on the back of my neck when I was in

there because there were so many orbs around me in those pictures. Unbelievable...loaded with spirits! There was tremendous unrest from the spirits, right time of the year, (around Halloween) where communication is between the two worlds.

Andy and I got a shot with a face in the mist shots of me and my wife Lizzy. You can see another face in the mist. It's the craziest thing and I could feel someone pushing on my shoulder as I was walking through the graveyard. When the people looked back at the pictures, they went from being skeptical to all of the sudden they were saying, "Oh, my God. What do we do?"

"You're fine where you're at...in a family graveyard at this time of the year. You're on a "ghost tour" and this stuff is real. If your senses can't pick it up through your neck and shoulders, you certainly can see the visual on the camera.

I told Andy that I was just going to set it all off if I went up there and I did! The people got what they paid for that night.

I don't think anybody slept very well that night in the mansion. Some even left early because the unrest and a little too much for them.

A lot of gravestones of kids, that never made it out of their teens, single years, and twenties, were out there. This was probably due to no cures at that time. Now, we have more technology and trained doctors.

Amazing stuff...visual evidence is pretty documentable.

*****

Physic Kids filmed at Burn Brae. I was not allowed to be anywhere in the house. Andy said that any interference I would bring could want to get in their way and throw everything off.

Phone interview with Mike Fraysse, the owner

Burn Brae Mansion is one of eight original mansions, but only three still exist today. They were built by the Mackenzie family who, at one time, were principals in the Singer Sewing Machine

Company. George Ross Mackenzie, who built these homes here, started with Singer in the assembly line as a cabinet maker and eventually became the president of the company. He built Singer into the richest corporation in the world by starting the payment plan back in the 1800s so that women could own sewing machines and be freed up instead of doing everything by hand.

They made so much money that they built these summer homes in the Hamlet of Glen Spey in New York State. It's about two hours outside of Manhattan and is right on the border of New York, New Jersey, and Pennsylvania; right off the Delaware River.

Mackenzie's people lived in Long Island and had their Singer sewing machine factories in New York City. Their summer homes spanned the entire mountain. The biggest mansion was George's mansion and had forty-five rooms. The smallest one is the one I own and it has twenty-seven rooms; it was built as a wedding present for his daughter.

I was an Olympic cycling coach and I wanted this house as a cycling training center.

After I bought it, I restored it back to what it was originally. At that time, it was divided into six apartments, one of the apartments that was upstairs used to be the servants' quarters.

There was a family that lived there by the name of Lovelace. The daughter was twelve-years-old and she used to tell stories about things that happened in her apartment. Because she was a little kid, we just thought that Hazel was making up stuff so she would sort of fit in to what Andy's acting crew was doing for Halloween.

They eventually had to move when she was only fourteen. The father was in his 80s and the mother in her 60s. It was just too much for them, the spiral staircase up to their apartment.

After they left, we started having other bike riders stay there and they would tell the same stories that Hazel told. They were here at different times and didn't know each other either personally, but they would say the same things as Hazel had.

We had ghost hunters come (many different groups) and with all of their tools. There was a person they would see all the time in the servants quarters. They all told the same story.

Around 4:30 in the morning, they would hear footsteps in the hallway and when they got up to look; they would see a woman in a white dress with long, blonde hair who would be sitting on these three steps that were between one level to another. The ghost hunters came to the conclusion she was a servant and mid-wife; she would birth all of the babies.

All of these different ghost hunters did not know each other but they all saw the same thing. After we had several groups here the town historian would look up old photos and history. Sure enough, right on my front lawn he found a picture with a woman in a long, white dress pushing a baby carriage.

It was exactly what the people had said.

We have a lot of guests come here and they would stay in the apartment. They hear the footsteps, a ball bouncing, cat crying in the attic (there is no cat in the attic), and all sorts of pictures of orbs. There were two pictures taken that actually have a face in the orb, which was just incredible! And besides that, there have been other instances reported of a man walking in and up the stairs from the main living area, to the second floor.

*****

People often say that the batteries run down quickly in cameras, flashlights and cell phones in the house. There is one area in particular where people also say that cell phones will be on when they turn it off and will be off when they turn it on and the dates will be changed on them. This section…used to be the nursery and in that particular part was also where babies had died back years ago, when many babies died. Back then, babies were born in houses because the whole idea of germs and sterilization wasn't very effective. People didn't want to go to the hospital for fear of getting sicker.

*****

Another building in the back of the main house, which was originally a stable, was where they used to bring the horses and carriages up the hill to the house. The bottom level was for the animals, second level was for the carriages, and top floor was for the hay loft.

It was turned into rooms many years later and was like a hotel. It had eighteen rooms which I rebuilt into twelve. It's like a stable, but each room has private bathrooms. When people stay there, first they hear voices but they see a vision of a man in overalls with a white tee shirt that paces around the building at night.

This has been going on for generations, as the previous owner's children tell me. Whether it was someone who was involved with the house here or before this house was built, or a caretaker; we don't know. He could have been a farmer who was here several hundred years ago.

*****

Whenever you take pictures you always find many, many orbs. You hear things, including voices.

*****

In the attic people always hear noises...sounds like people are playing ball or moving furniture. It's a big, big attic but there's never anybody there.

*****

Historians found a picture and history of the original plantation. The picture shows Mackenzie's prize Arabian stallions. The man holding them was wearing the same overalls and white shirt, but it doesn't mean it was him.

137

*****

There was a fourteen-year-old girl who visited here that, from the time she was born, she could see people and their auras. She knew good people from bad people. She didn't feel good the whole time she was at the mansion. She felt great when she came in but she couldn't sleep. The next day when she left, she got into the car and as they drove away a couple of miles, she felt better.

*****

Living here doesn't bother me at all. I hear noises and see flashes and other things all the time. All the ghost hunters here said that all the energy here is positive; nothing negative or bad here...it's all good.

*****

The woman that we bought the house from heard what everyone was saying and she started talking about things. She had kept it all to herself because she didn't want people to think she was crazy. She would even tell her husband and he told her she was nuts. They moved here in 1969 and from the time I bought the house in 1993, she always thought that the house did not like her.

Things that would happen to her here did not happen to anybody else. The washing machine would be on and she would go down and it would be off. The stove would not work until she turned it off, but it worked normal for everyone else.

I let them stay here when we had the closing for the house; a couple more weeks for them to pack up. I had to get everything ready. I was going to restore the whole house and she said that after we had the closing, she went back to the house...her husband was outside doing something and she was sitting downstairs in the living room area. She heard crazy laughter! She looked around and there was nobody there. She said, "What is it, what is it?" and she heard "I won!"

I asked one of the ghost hunters, "Why would that be?"

They really didn't know but they thought it was probably because of the restoration. It was chopped up into lots of apartments and the spirits didn't like it. I had no problems because I restored it back to what it was. They're back to living where they used to live, the way they found it.

There have been three different families that lived in this house since the original family. The Mackenzie daughter married a man named Elkin, and they had four children. The family after them also had four kids. When the Physic Kids were here they got the feeling of four kids playing in the attic. Four...always four... (They knew nothing about the mansion.) Growing up, most kids play in the attic.

In the 1800s, the original Elkin kids died and were buried out back in the cemetery.

*****

When I bought the house there was an old couple from Ukraine who lived in one of the apartments. When they came here, after World War II, this was the second place they lived.

She died in the fall of 2005 and he died shortly after... They were married over seventy-five years. She died in the house and he died in the hospital and were very close to each other. I asked Chip Coffey from Paranormal States if he died in the hospital, how could he end up back here? Chip explained that when someone dies, the energy from that person or spirit wants to be with their loved one.

She baked all the time and the house always smelled of baked goods. When the girls from Physic Kids were here they said that when they walked upstairs, all they could smell was chocolate chip cookies and baked stuff. The kitchen wasn't even there anymore. The man was a music composer and he was a conductor in the church choir. The girls also heard classical music.

In the big, curved glass windows they visualized an old couple sitting there by in the alcove, looking out. The couple used to sit there, each by a different window with a card table between them and do puzzles together.

So if you drive past this house at night, you just might see two people sitting in the windows.

Chapter 19
Mile High Grill & Inn

309 Main Street
Mailing Address: PO Box 1311, Jerome Arizona 86331
Inn Reservation Phone: 928-634-5094
Email: Restaurant at: milehighgrill@yahoo.com
Website: http://www.jeromemilehighinn.com/
Jet Tennant & Liz Gale, owners

History
Jet and Liz, Social Workers by trade, they fled Phoenix to the small mountain town of Jerome, Arizona; it captured their hearts.

With Jet's ability to make tasty food and Liz's enthusiasm, we decided to go into the restaurant business. After spotting a place on Main Street Jet and Liz opened their first restaurant, the Red Rooster Café.

Four years later and with much success, they moved up the street to a more central location on Main Street; bigger space, expanded menu and opened the Mile High Grill and Inn. They brought with them dedication to fresh ingredients, putting a fun twist to traditional favorites. They like to say that they are, "Americana with a southwestern flare!"

The Mile High Grill & Inn has been in operation for five years.

It's located in Klinkstall and the building has been in continuous operation since 1899.

Ghost Stories
Interview with Jet Tennant

People hear noises of a doorknob turning, but it's a little chair at the top of the stairs, turning by itself.

I don't go up there at night. As you walk back there is feels light, but as you get closer it feels dark.

I have researched and can't find anything on it.

I think it may have been a mortuary...but no proof.

*****

I have seen people out of the corner of my eye. I thought someone had let somebody in without telling me. But, not true.

*****

I saw a guy laying on the bed and thought I had let someone in early. But, that impression in the bed sheet is still there. He does this all the time.

*****

The inn burned down in its location two times.

We think this is an elderly woman that started the fires. We have since put up eighteen-inch concrete walls. Now it's a solid building.

*****

The Mexican dishwasher in the kitchen got kissed on the cheek and could smell perfume. The Mexicans will not work upstairs...they walk up and walk out. We try not to promote ghosts because of that.

*****

One night I was working by myself in the building and had to go to the bathroom. It's good I had already done my business because when I got ready to leave I noticed that there was a stain on the door. Then I heard a loud knock, raping, and bamb bamb! This has happened a lot.

*****

A couple, from England, came to visit. They heard cats all night. They said that the inn was beautiful and comfortable, but they will never be back.

There is way more activity towards the back of the inn.

*****

We get a lot of cat stories times, from totally different people. Come to think of it, there was a cat that died in one of the fires. Maybe he brought along his friends!

Chapter 20
Inn at Merridun

Peggy, Assistant Innkeeper
100 Merridun Place
Union, South Carolina 29379
(864) 427-7052 888-892-6020
Website: http://www.merridun.com/welcome.html

History

Merridun, an antebellum mansion listed on the National Register of Historic Places, is surrounded by shady oaks and century-old magnolias and is located in the gently rolling upstate region of South Carolina. The nine-acre property is located in the tranquil community of Union, South Carolina. The mansion, although very secluded, is only three to four blocks from the main section of downtown Union.

Now one of the most regal homes in this city of colonnaded mansions, the originally Georgian styled house was built in 1855-57 by William Keenan, a local merchant and mayor of Union in 1855. The property at that time included four thousand acres and was known as Keenan Plantation.

The house and property were acquired in 1876 by Benjamin

H. Rice, a local Union lawyer. He had inherited a plantation in the Buffalo area known as Pleasant Grove, which adjoined the Keenan property.

At the time of purchase, the house in Union became their town home on this eight thousand acre estate; cotton was the main industry of the plantation. Some major renovations were done to the home in the early 1880s.

In the Early 1880s Thomas Cary Duncan (1862-1928), son of Bishop W.W. Duncan and Medora Rice Duncan, moved to Union to live and work with his grandfather, B.H. Rice. In 1885 T.C. Duncan brought his bride Fannie Merriman (1863-1948) of Greenwood, South Carolina to live in Union. T.C. Duncan inherited the house from his maternal grandparents and renamed it "Merridun"—a combination of three family names that graced this ancestral home (Merriman, Rice, Duncan).

In 1893, T.C. Duncan almost single-handedly restored Union to its former position of wealth and prestige by introducing the textile industry to the city. He built the first successful cotton mill within sight of this mansion. A political and industrial leader, he served in the South Carolina House of Representatives from 1892-94 and 1916-18 and is also responsible for constructing the mill in Buffalo, Union's B.U.C. Railroad and hydro-electric plant.

After inheriting Merridun T.C. Duncan "remodeled" giving the originally patterned Georgian style exterior its characteristics of the classic revival style. The original plain double piazzas with Doric columns were replaced with Corinthian columns and side wing marble porticos were added, resulting in over 2400 square feet of porch space.

The 7900 square feet Georgian floor plan includes a stunning curved staircase, large foyers on both floors, a music room, parlor, library, dining room, kitchen, seven bedrooms, multiple bathrooms, and a third story cupola. A brick wing behind the main house once was used as servant's kitchen, well, laundry house, quarters and a smoke house.

The carriage barn, located behind the brick wing, still houses the Duncan's carriage; plans for restoration are underway. Unique architectural aspects of this mansion include frescoed ceilings in the music room and dining room, mosaic tiles and turn-of-the-century stenciling and faux graining in the main foyer and beautiful chandeliers.

T.C. and Fannie Duncan had two sons (both died at a very young age) and 3 daughters: Medora Eleanor Duncan Fitten (1887-1960), Louisa Merriman Duncan Eaves (1890-1975), and Fannie Merriman Duncan (1897-1974). Medora married and moved to Atlanta; Louisa and Fannie lived at Merridun until their deaths. Louisa's only son, Thomas Cary Duncan Eaves and his wife Juliet Caruana Eaves, inherited Merridun; seven generations of the Benjamin Rice family enjoyed the pleasures of Merridun prior to being sold in the summer of 1990.

Portraits of Thomas Cary Duncan and his wife, Fannie Merriman Duncan hang in the foyer and parlors.

Ghost Stories
Phone interview with Peggy, owner

We Arrived in October of 1990. We would see lots of pennies on the floor but have not seen any spirits. I was in the Navy at one time and stationed in North Carolina. We had a house in Raleigh (as well as this one) and when we were spending the night, I did see a spirit twice. They were probably about eight or nine months apart. Part of my scientific mind says I don't believe the other part knows that since I've been here there's no doubt that things exist.

I get lots of questions; if I'm afraid to live in this big, old house by myself. I say "No, I'm more afraid of the living than I am of the dead."

No doubt things exist. If I hear strange things, I just get up, go down and check it out. My ex-husband did see things when he lived here and my brother did as we were restoring the house. He has seen things in the house as well as a Civil War soldier outside of the house.

Guests come as there are more and more after television shows. They want to see a ghost. I've never seen anything although I have heard and felt things I can't explain. If I could make them appear on demand, I'd be a very rich woman!

*****

Some of our guests go away disappointed at not having experiences, and some go away very happy because they have lots of orbs on their pictures, or they heard something. I have many people come with video cameras and things. I'll get emails a week later telling me the things they caught on camera or heard. They'll say, "Has anyone ever mentioned whistling upstairs in the hallway or marbles rolling on a floor?"

*****

We had a cat that was part of our home; his name was JD and passed away when he was sixteen and one half years.

This guest asked me twice; "Did JD ever bother the Christmas decorations that were on the doorknobs?"

I told her he did; on occasion cats like strings and things. She said that twice in one day she had heard tinkle of bells from the doorknob and it woke her up.

We've had other guests, since he died, that have orbs in their pictures at cat level instead of people level or up in the air. Several people think his spirit is still alive here. He occasionally comes to visit me in the night. He jumps up on the bed. I wish he would come back for good.

*****

We had a clairvoyant that came here a couple of times during the 90's to visit and identified ten energy forces during her visits.

She thought that Mr. and Mrs. Duncan were still here. Their job was to guide us in the restoration of the house.

*****

When we bought the house and were flying back to California, we actually named all the rooms and picked the colors out for the wallpaper. We came back and to start working on the house and when we peeled back the layers of old wallpaper, we noticed that the colors we had picked were the originally on the walls.

We have a room upstairs that my painters call the Pepto-Bismol room…very Victorian, very feminine and very pink.

*****

There's a lady here by the name of Margaret, we don't know who she is. She has red hair and there is usually a little, white dog with her. Over the years I have had lots of experiences with a small animal, this was before JD died.

*****

The main stairs, where people tend to see things (including my ex-husband and my brother) MaryAnn. She apparently was a spinster of one of the former owners. The clairvoyant said that her job hers was to be my guardian spirit. She thought I worked too hard and she thought that I should slow down and that another of her favorite things to do was harass my ex-husband.

*****

I have a gentleman staying here now on a long-term basis who is helping me with some restoration things while he's also restoring another house here in town. He hears people knocking on the foot of the bed and impressions of someone sitting on the bed.

So he comes down in the morning and sometimes tells me about those things. He gets a little spooked but not scared; he's seen ghosts before so he was not scared.

*****

We also found two Native Americans in the house. We are probably on Indian burial grounds.

*****

We have two children in the house. I have not experienced them so much but I've had guests who occasionally hear children playing and talking. I have a lady from North Carolina who is a frequent visitor who basically carries on a conversation with a whole family that does include children. She does a lot of audio taping and that sort of thing and plays with the children.

*****

The tenth one that the clairvoyant identified was (I'm going to call her "Nanny".) She seems to be seen on the outside only. Her job here was to guard all children here at the inn. They think she might have been Mrs. Duncan's nanny or mammy or something like that. I have had several people over the years identify someone on the back portion on the outside of the house. We haven't figured out who she is.

*****

Over the last five years we have more and more people coming. They tend to identify more than ten people. People are seen on the front porch and at different parts of the house.

*****

The lady that comes and talks to the whole family on my third floor, which is actually the fourth floor storage room people who have supposedly worked here but not at the same time. It's a mother that has four children, an older woman and then a gentleman that were here; but not all in the same time-frame. She carries on great conversations and originally it was the tape, but now she just talks with them. I take all of this with a grain of salt. I don't have that knack of talking with dead people. Occasionally I see the things out of the corner of your eye I just dismiss those things.

149

*****

We smell old rose perfume and a cigar; sometimes separately, sometimes together.

*****

Three or four years ago I had my mother come and visit during the holidays with both of my brothers; we did a lot of decorating. (I hear more from my intercom, which is interesting.)

One night about 1:00 AM, I heard the sound of music; laughing and talking. I got up and went to the top of the stairs and didn't hear anything so I went downstairs (I knew mother was asleep in her room... she wasn't partying.)

One of brothers was asleep on the couch so I made my way, being sure that the house was locked up and there was nobody in the house. Then I went back upstairs. Two more times during that night I came back down the stairs. I could hear music going on, but of course I never saw anything. It seems like somebody was having a party and forgot to invite me!

*****

Some of rooms are in the old ballroom on the second floor. Spirits tend to that floor

*****

I have a guest, a business woman, who came to visit for years. One night she called me again and wanted to book a room, but said that she didn't want to stay in "Lucy's" room.

So when she got here, I asked if she could tell me why she didn't want to stay in that room. She said that she didn't get much sleep. A lady by the name of "Francis" showed up and, of course, that's one of the old family names here. She said to me, "You know that this is the coat room for the ballroom.

I said, "Well, no I didn't. So she said that the spirits proceeded throughout the night to bring guests in to introduce them to her.

Now, these are things I wish would happen to me, Francis.

*****

We have people that hear Indian drums that I have not heard. Actually, the lady who talks to the family hears them.

Probably about her second or third time she visited on her audio tape she said to them, Peggy says she's never seen anything here. The response back was "She doesn't need to, she knows we're here."

*****

We just sort of co-exist but they're not harmful. I have had guests here that have heard doors opening and closing and people moving furniture. They would come down and ask if we were moving furniture during the night? No...

They would go lift up the rugs because they just knew there would be marks on the floor where people had been moving the furniture.

*****

The person called MaryAnn is the one that is most often seen. People can describe her dress and things down to the fabric. People who see her say that they never see her face.

The former owner came back shortly after we opened with a lunch group. She was telling people stories that had happened to her. That was a real common spirit for them to see when they were here and she said it was probably a person named MaryAnn.

She and her friends, aunts, and mother in law would be playing bridge and would say, "Why isn't the lady in the corner joining us?"

*****

We have also experienced a male presence in the house. The lady said that once her grandchildren had said that they had seen a man in grandma's room but the children were young and they chose not to get into that because the boys would be afraid at night.

*****

We occasionally get guests here because they have heard of our ghost stories. One day we had a couple here looking for a haunting. Another couple overhead the young couple talking about the hauntings and they checked out immediately. They had just had a demonic experience and they had had enough of that.

*****

Our guests have lots of little things like a picture falling off the wall and landing on its corner and this heavy picture did not break.

Chapter 21
Hotel St. Nicholas

303 N. 3rd Street
P.O. Box 1459
Cripple Creek, Colorado 80813
719-689-0856 888-786-4857

Website: http://www.hotelstnicholas.com/hsncontactus.html

The Hotel St. Nicholas has enjoyed a long and colorful history. The hotel traces its roots to the year 1898 and its construction, by the Catholic Sisters of Mercy, as the first dedicated general hospital to serve Cripple Creek, Colorado, and the surrounding area at the height of the 1890's Gold Rush.

History

The Catholic Order of the Sisters of Mercy has a rich history of over 175 years. The Order was founded by Catherine McAuley in Dublin, Ireland, in 1831. McAuley, born into a prosperous Catholic family in 1778, was orphaned at age 19. For several years Catherine, a devout Catholic, lived with relatives who disapproved of her practice of Catholicism. Within several years they suffered financial losses themselves, making it necessary for

Catherine to find outside employment and residence.

She soon entered the household of William and Catherine Callaghan, elderly and prosperous Quakers, as a household manager and companion to Mrs. Callaghan. During the next 20 years and while remaining with the Callaghans, Catherine became deeply involved in ministering to the needy, particularly poor women and children who were often overlooked by other institutions of the day. In 1822, following the death of the Callaghans,

Catherine inherited their £25,000 estate (worth about $1 million today), and in 1827 opened the first House of Mercy, in Dublin, as a home providing religious, educational and social services to disadvantaged women and girls.

Although McAuley originally intended to establish a secular society, her work and advice from supportive Dublin clergy led her and two associates to profess vows in December, 1831, and establish the Religious Institute of the Sisters of Mercy. In the early 1800's there were few social support organizations for the poor, and the need was great. Sisters of Mercy members soon became known as the "walking nuns" because of the frequency with which they were seen moving throughout Dublin ministering to the sick and poor. By the time of McAuley's death in 1841 there were ten foundations in Ireland and England with over 100 sisters.

The first Sisters of Mercy arrived in the United States from Ireland in 1843 at the invitation of the Bishop of Pittsburgh, Pennsylvania. Their energy in ministering to the sick and poor in the new world attracted many new members. By 1854, Sisters from Ireland had settled in New York and San Francisco, and continued to spread throughout the country, establishing schools and hospitals.

In 1882, at the request of the Bishop of Colorado and Utah, Joseph Machebeuf,

Mother Mary John Baptist Meyers led a group of five sisters from St. Louis to Colorado to establishing a hospital and school in Durango, and in 1887 in Ouray, Colorado. By 1889 they were working in Denver. In 1894, Sister Mary Claver Coleman was sent to Cripple Creek to establish the town's first general hospital.

The Sisters originally operated from an existing wood-framed building at 326 E. Eaton, one block from the current St. Nicholas, and served three hundred and seven patients during their first year. A massive fire in April, 1896 destroyed most of Cripple Creek, and led to an incident of drama and irony.

As the fire progressed through Cripple Creek, many wooden-framed buildings were dynamited in an effort to slow the fire. While the sisters were evacuating patients to safer locations, a member of an anti-catholic society entered the hospital's kitchen and attempted to destroy the building by placing dynamite in the stove chimney.

To the man's misfortune, the dynamite exploded prematurely, causing little damage to the hospital, but blowing off his leg. He was evacuated with the other patients, and the compassionate care he received from the Sisters led him to express remorse for his deed. His shoe, which had landed in the tea kettle, was kept by the Sisters as a memento.

Although the original hospital survived, the fire convinced the Sisters that there was a need for a more modern and safer structure. The Sisters engaged John J. Huddart, a well known Denver architect responsible for many Colorado landmarks, to develop a design. Huddart's design was an elegant three-story brick structure that mixed elements of several design styles to create a stately and distinctive building. Construction of the current St. Nicholas was begun in 1896 and was completed in

1898, at a cost of $12,000. The first two floors of the hospital were used for patients.

The Sisters' living quarters were on the 3rd floor. The hospital orderly occupied the attic. The St. Nicholas took advantage of Cripple Creek's developing town infrastructure, which was advanced for its day. The new hospital was "thoroughly modern, with electric lights, steam heat, hot and cold running water, and a surgery department." Dedicated on May 15, 1898, the hospital was in use from March 12, 1898, when it received its first patient, a young miner named Elijah

Ayers, who had fallen down a shaft at the Specimen Mine. The hospital was named for and dedicated by then Colorado Bishop Nicholas Matz. In 1902 an addition was made to the hospital to serve as additional living quarters for the sisters.

After almost thirty years of service, the Sisters left Cripple Creek in 1924, and the hospital was purchased and operated privately by a series of local doctors. During the years as mines closed and the population of Cripple Creek shrank, the hospital continued to serve the area.

The St. Nicholas Hotel continues to host guests who were born or treated in the hospital during the mid-1900's, or whose family or friends were. The hospital finally closed in 1972, and was used as a boarding house or stood vacant until its purchase and meticulous refurbishment in 1995, when it joined the list of fine Cripple Creek hotels as the Hotel St. Nicholas.

Spirits and Ghosts

Cripple Creek, with its wild and turbulent past, has a history of unexplained, supernatural occurrences that has led it to be called "one of the most haunted towns in America". Tales of haunted Cripple Creek hotels, casinos, and homes abound. Maggie, who inhabits the top floor at the Colorado Grande Casino, may be the best know of Cripple Creek's ghostly residents, but many of the area's turn-of-the-century businesses and homes have a history of strange sights and sounds that offer no apparent rational explanation.

*****

The Hotel St. Nicholas is no exception. Since its reopening in 1995, a number of unexplained events have happened at the hotel, and it seems that at least two friendly, but mischievous spirits, call the hotel home.

One has been identified as Petey, who on some occasions has moved small items or hidden cigarettes in the bar. Petey is believed to be the spirit of a young boy, possibly an orphan, who was cared for by the Sisters of Mercy in the St. Nicholas' early days.

*****

A second ghost, dressed as a miner, has been reportedly heard and seen walking down the back stairways, or seen sitting on a stool in the hotel office.

*****

While these two spirits seem to be the most common, an occasional report of other sightings or 'feelings' comes in from other areas of the hotel. Regardless of the number, the St. Nicholas' spirits seem to be a friendly and playful, if elusive, group.

The Hotel St. Nicholas has hosted a number of ghost hunting groups on several occasions.

Chapter 22
Beardslee Castle

123 Old State Road
Little Falls, New York 13365

315-823-3000 800-487-5861

Website: http://www.beardsleecastle.com/

History

In 1781 John Beardslee left Connecticut in search of a fortune. He was a practiced architect, civil engineer and mechanic.

In 1787 he arrived at Whitestown, New York where he built mills financed by the sale of shares, later selling his portion at a tidy profit. With the success of this project he was engaged by the state to build a series of Mills for the Oneida Indians.

Mr. Beardslee's construction jobs continued and between 1790 and 1796 he built the first bridge across the Mohawk at Little Falls, the old red mill at Little Falls, mills at Van Hornesville and Canajoharie, bridges at West Canada Creek, East Canada Creek and Fort Plain, and the Herkimer County Courthouse and Jail.

He settled at East Creek, about a mile up from the Mohawk, where a small town grew up around his developments. Known as

Beardslee Mills or Beardslee City, the settlement thrived and grew to over 2000 residents in the early 1800's.

When the Erie Canal was built, bringing the majority of trade to the south side of the river, Beardslee Mills fell into hard times, later to be abandoned altogether. John Beardslee died in October of 1825, the same month the Canal opened. All that remains of Beardslee's City is an overgrown graveyard at the edge of a cornfield and the limestone Beardslee family mausoleum in a stand of virgin pine along the East Creek.

John's son Augustus lived to an old age and carried on the Beardslee tradition of hard work and individual accomplishment. He graduated Union college in 1821 and went on to a fruitful law practice in Little Falls, later elected to the State Legislature as well as serving time as a member of the judiciary. He was selected by Lincoln as one of several representatives to a convention in Virginia in efforts to stave off Civil War.

Augustus managed the family fortune well, investing in New York Central Railroad. When he built the Castle in 1860 a covered walkway was constructed leading to the East Creek station and a private semaphore installed so he could stop trains to travel to New York. The Beardslee's borrowed heavily on designs of Irish Castles in constructing their home. Helen Caitlin Bernard Beardslee outlived her husband by a quarter century and continued to add artifacts and additions to the Castle.

Augustus's son, Guy Roosevelt Beardslee, was born in 1858. He was schooled locally as a child, later attending Charlier Institute in New York and then spending two years studying in France. He was appointed to West Point Military Academy barely graduating four years later, last in his class, in 1879. He received a commission in the infantry assigned to Fort Niobrara in Nebraska shortly after the General Custer incident. He resigned his commission one year later to return to East Creek to handle the family estate.

He took his place managing the estate that included a full working farm, cheese factory, and sawmill. In 1892 two engineers approached him from a firm in New York who paid him $40,000 in return for an option to develop power at East Creek on property still owned at the old Beardslee City.

They were unable to raise enough capital for the project, which was considered risky because of the need to transmit power over the distance of three miles to the nearest town.

Drawing on his own engineering background and enlisting the service of John Cairns, Guy undertook the project himself, with the intent of mechanizing the family farm. This was to become the first rural electric power in the country.

He realized the commercial potential and soon contracted several local farms as customers for the surplus power, later adding customers to the east in the towns of St. Johnsville, Fort Plain, Nelliston and Canajoharie. The power to St. Johnsville was turned on on St. Patrick's Day 1898. In 1911 Mr. Beardslee sold the business to Adirondack Power and Light, which later became Niagara Mohawk or NIMO.

With the success and sale of the power company, the Beardslee's led a comfortable life, vacationing in Europe and spending winters in Florida and Mexico. It was while vacationing in Florida in February of 1919 that tragedy struck the Beardslee's. In the early hours of the morning a fire started in the front of the Castle.

The structure was completely gutted leaving nothing but the stone walls. The newspaper of Feb. 19th claimed the cause was arson to cover-up theft. A 'mysterious man' had been seen in the area for a few days before the blaze. The reports noted that all the precious artifacts and furnishings gathered from the Beardslee's world travels were destroyed.

Only the main floor was rebuilt, leaving the second floor without a roof and with railings across the window openings. The back of the building was turned into garden space, the stone walls draped with flowers and vines. Two of the original three tunnels, which connected the buildings on the estate, were closed off and the rooms they led into were sealed forever. The Beardslee's continued to share their time between New York and Florida until 1937 when Guy passed away. He was survived by his wife but left no children. Ethel died in 1941 to be laid to rest beside her husband in the family mausoleum at East Creek.

Ethel's sister, Gertrude Shriver, sold the estate to Adam Horn of St. Johnsville, who took up residence with his wife for one year. They soon sold the building and Carriage House to Anton 'Pop' Christensen of St. Johnsville who opened the estate to the public as 'The Manor'. The name was to stick for forty-five years.

Pop and his wife resided in a small cottage built beside the Castle in what is now our west courtyard. AS pop grew older he became terminally ill. After many thwarted attempts he commi6tted suicide by hanging himself in the ladies room of the Castle in what is now the side entrance foyer. Most of the Beardslee furnishings wee still intact at that time, but the Christensen's daughters sold them at auction a few years later before selling the building to Herkimer restaurateur John Dedla.

The fire broke out in the back of the kitchen during the early morning hours of August 30, 1989. By the time the firemen arrived the fire had spread through the entire kitchen. When the smoke cleared over 1500 square feet of kitchen area had been destroyed.

The building was abandoned, became a hangout for late night parties, and anything not bolted down was stolen. All the while the water flowed, down the slope behind the castle (and off what was left of the roof) with every drop flowing through the burnt out kitchen door into the dining rooms. The vines grew up over the roofline and worked their tendrils into the roof causing even more leaks. Two spring lines in the cellar burst and constant trickle of water began that did not stop for three more years.

The castle was purchased by the current owners and renovated for a reopening in 1994 as "Beardslee Castle", changing the name to "Castle" out of respect for the Beardslee's original intents. After being abandoned for three years it took nearly 18 months of cleaning and restoration to return it to its original state. Nearly every square inch of the Castle has been restored or rebuilt.

The original oak parquet floors, covered for the preceding twenty years with wall-to-wall carpeting have been returned to their glistening shine. The stonework interior with its wide gothic arches have been thoroughly hand cleaned of 140 years of dirt and soot. The wood paneled ceilings have been restored to a warm luster highlighted by art deco and mission style lighting fixtures. The second floor banquet room features beautiful floor-to-ceiling plate glass windows giving a panoramic view of the valley. A completely new kitchen services all three floors.

Ghost Stories

In the mid 1700's, during the French and Indian War, a fortified homestead stood on the property where the Castle is now located. The Mohawk Valley was the central supply point for militia along the northern borders of the colonies. Munitions and powder were stored at the homestead. Late one night a band of Indians crept into the home and made their way into the tunnels where the munitions were stored. Legend has it their torches ignited the powder and the Indians were blown to bits.

Could their spirits, here long before the Castle, still linger here?

*****

The Indian Connection Indian activity was heavy through the Mohawk Valley in pre-colonial times. The same waterfalls that Guy Beardslee harnessed for electric power were held in awe as a symbol of the Great Spirit on Earth by the local Mohawks.

*****

A major camp in use over a period of almost 400 years was located just a few hundred yards to our east, along a knoll that overlooks the Mohawk. The spot can be seen just as you cross the East Creek bridge heading east on the right side of the road. Some psychic researchers point to the Indians as a source for restless psychic energy.

*****

Another possible source of Indian presence was brought about by Guy Beardslee himself. After graduating West Point, Guy Beardslee was commissioned in the Army and assigned to Fort Niobrara in Nebraska where the Army was setting outposts to take over land from the Sioux. Whether Mr. Beardslee ever saw battle with the Sioux is unknown. However he did return to East Creek with at least three full Sioux war bonnets and a collection of tomahawks, knives, and other ceremonial artifacts.

Sioux war artifacts are held sacred and their mere presence in a building could have profound effects, especially if they had been taken in battle. All of the Indian artifacts were destroyed when the building burned in 1919.

*****

Lights, Lights, Lights In the early 50's, travelers along Route 5, reported seeing a bright yellow or blue light that would rush out at their cars from the trees or chase them down the road. The light was reported as blinding at times, other times seen in the distance floating through the woods. Several fatal accidents occurred along the bend in the road where the light was reported. One surviving woman reported that the light rushed out from the trees and blinded her husband, the driver, who perished in the wreck. Other drivers reported seeing a young child walking along the roadside late at night. In just the past 6 years since the Castle reopened we have had four incidents of cars driving off the road in a perfectly clear, straight stretch less than 1/4 mile long in front of the Castle.

An extension of this legend a story spread of the ghost of Mr. Beardslee walking the grounds holding a lantern with a blue light, searching for a lost child who had either drowned in a pond or pool or had been hit by an oncoming train. Many reported seeing the light of the lantern. A grand-daughter of Pop Christensen has reported seeing the lantern floating on its own behind the building.

*****

The Mausoleum... In the mid sixties the ghost stories peaked as the Beardslee Family Mausoleum at the edge of Beardslee City cemetery became a popular late night party spot for young people. Partygoers reported seeing strange lights at the Mausoleum as well as hearing voices.

The stories turned to tragedy when a few individuals broke into the Beardslee crypt and desecrated the graves. A Little Falls resident was later arrested and the skull of Augustus Beardslee was found in his closet.

The mausoleum still exists far back in the woods among a stand of 200 foot tall virgin pine trees. Beer cans from the sixties are still scattered here and there as if untouched by time. The pines open around the crypt to leave it in sunlight most of the day and although rarely visited anymore, no weeds grow in the path that leads to the entrance. We were sent a photograph that had been taken at the crypt by a Syracuse police officer. A strange rainbow appears at the side of the photo that does not follow the regular pattern of colors of the spectrum. The police crime lab was unable to explain the appearance of the colors in the photo.

*****

Ghosts of the eighties In 1983 the owner of Beardslee Manor decided to find out if there was any truth to the ghost stories... along with over forty reporters from newspapers, magazines, TV, and radio. Norm Gauthier, a ghost hunter from the New Hampshire Institute for Paranormal Research arrived with a car load of equipment to test for ghosts.

During the course of the night tape recorders would run for ten minute stretches. Incense was lit to attract the spirits. At the end of the night the tapes were played back and faint voices were heard whispering...some almost playful in nature. Mr. Gauthier's conclusion was that the Manor was definitely haunted and by at least two spirits.

*****

Who are they? Many people have identified a young woman, dressed in white who has been seen on the grounds sitting, walking, or standing by a window. Popular legend has named her 'Abigail" and suggested she was a bride who died the night before her wedding.

The origin of this story is unknown although several weddings did take place at the Castle when it was a residence. More than one psychic challenged with identifying the resident spirits have felt the presence of the woman, dressed in a white dress with a high collar and bottom sleeves.

One person in particular who was unfamiliar with the property or stories of the past identified this woman further saying that she was fond of fabrics, flowers, and most of all the Castle, and that she remained here because she loved the building. During construction, two people witnessed a very strong smell of ladies perfume in the empty Carriage House.

*****

The first owner of the Castle as a restaurant, Pop Christensen, hung himself in the building following a protracted illness. His family then sold off most of the original Beardslee furnishings that were left on the property. Could his spirit haunt the restaurant?

*****

Other stories seem to follow a more sinister line. One night a few staff members were playing with a Ouija board when the lights suddenly went out and a tremendous force hit one of them in the chest and pushed him across the room.

*****

Tales of overturned tables and chairs that were found when the first employees arrived in the morning... silverware flying around the room, bottles and glasses breaking...all sorts of physical activities. Several staff members reported hearing disembodied unintelligible voices all around them floating through the air. Sharp whispers of someone's name...as if from a fellow staff member.

*****

Three employees were chased from the building late one night by a thunderous scream or howl that seemed to come from all around them at once. Music was sometimes heard coming from the second floor.

More recently staff members have heard the sound of a lady singing on the second floor, sounds of doors opening and closing, footsteps across the main floor hall are heard from below in the bar after everyone has left the dining rooms, and even sounds of keys jingling.

A former staff member who had moved to Florida was back in the area and decided to take some pictures to show his friends what the Castle looked like. When he returned to Florida and had the roll developed the form of a shadowy figure with an expression of dismay was plainly visible covering the entire frame. No one has been able to explain the unusual appearance in the photo.

Most recently a couple traveling past the castle were horrified when a young lady stepped out into the road. The car struck the woman according to the couple and witnesses in a car traveling the opposite direction. The police were called and although all three parties checked along the road in the area of the accident, there was no woman to be found and no marks on the car.

*****

Strange Feelings…In 1984 the cathedral ceiling that had been open to the second floor was closed off and some of the activity seemed to subside. Still the main evidence for haunting was something that no one could see, hear, or feel.

The strongest evidence was that the place felt haunted. Once the staff had finished cleaning at the end of the night and had gone downstairs nobody would dare to go back upstairs alone. Certain rooms and places were regarded as more haunted than others and newcomers could identify these as easily as a long-time staff member.

A psychic, who was consulted in New York City, many miles away, was able to pinpoint much of the activity to areas where water was present… as well as identify the water problems that plagued the building for years, possibly indicating that spirits dwell in the water…a belief held by Native Americans. One of these spots became fairly well known for stopping watches and keeping cameras from functioning… the same spot where the mysterious ghost photograph was later taken.

*****

We have spoken to many former staff members who had stopped in at the burned out Castle after the 1989 fire. Although the building was unlocked and wide open, they all felt that something would not permit them to enter.

Indeed, one strong theory is that the ghosts were abused by the storytelling and ghost hunting. Perhaps the spirits had something to do with the fire as an attempt to drive out the restaurateurs. Strangely enough when the flames were finally out, the entire kitchen both upstairs and down was destroyed without burning a single square foot of the original structure.

We leave it to you to explore the Castle and judge for yourself whether it 'feels' haunted. Perhaps you'll have an experience of a ghostly nature too. One thing is for certain, Augustus Beardslee's Castle is a beautiful and compelling building that has a powerful, true sense of place. Unique, captivating and mysterious as well, we are honored to share the Castle with our guests, from this dimension and any other.

Chapter 23
The Beal House Inn, Bar, and Restaurant

Catherine Keller, Innkeeper
2 West Main Street
Littleton, New Hampshire 03561
603-444-2661
Website: http://www.thebealhouseinn.com/
www.thebealhouseinn.com

History

Built in 1833 as a farm by the Flanders Family, the house now looks nothing like the original. The now Inn, was the main house and the porch was a walkway to the now restaurant that was the carriage barn. The transformations are occurring to this very day with building renovations and owner changes, but the character of this great place has remained the same and true to its history.

The home, then located at 247 Main St, changed ownership after the original man-of-the-house Nathaniel Flanders died in 1897, his son George Flanders born in Littleton in 1861, sold the family farm to George Morse in 1904. Kate Morse after being widowed sold the home to Martha Cushman in 1932, who then sold it to Justus and Marjorie Beal in 1939.

The inn was then opened and operated by Mrs. Beal. The inn

even then, had a reputation for elegance and style while maintaining the welcoming family feel. When Mr. Justus Beal died in 1944, Marjorie continued to run the inn and later remarried to Edward Grady in 1950. The inn was run and operated by Mr. and Mrs. Edward Grady until they retired and sold the business in 1985.

Although the building has changed hands in 1988, 1990, 1991, 1995, 1997, 2001, 2006, 2008, and now 2009, and foreclosed on twice, the inn and now restaurant still maintain that same feel that Mrs. Beal created back in 1939; Elegance, sophistication, welcoming, charming, and peaceful.

The now eleven bedroom inn still sees visitors coming from around the globe and the three-star rated restaurant receives raves from equal distances.

The Ghost Stories
Phone interview with Catherine Keller, Innkeeper

We moved down to the hotel and stayed in the Beal Room. The first few nights were okay. Then after about six nights my little tea-cup Chihuahua kept barking towards the bedroom while we were in the sitting room.

I couldn't figure out what she wanted, so I went back and she still wouldn't go. I didn't see anything; I thought she was just barking at me. She is temperamental but she doesn't usually bark. I let it go and held her a little bit on the couch.

That night, I was trying to put her in her little cage with her baby blanket. She wouldn't go in the room alone. I went in the room and put her in the cage and she kept growling. I thought, "What in the world? Now, you behave yourself."

Shortly thereafter I went to bed and I wasn't sleeping because she kept growling. All of the sudden I looked up and there was something that looked like a cloud. But, I could see it was a woman in a long dress. It scared the living daylights out of me. Then she went away

This happened for a couple of nights and my dog would still not go into that bedroom by herself.

A couple of nights later, I saw a woman at the top of the steps with a dog. The dog looked very vicious; it kept growling. My dog kept scratching to get out of her cage.

That happened a few times and one night it came to me and then just went away. It happened to me before in Memphis, except it was a man. I don't know if it followed me or what.

A few weeks later, I moved to the third floor and nothing happened for weeks, then all of the sudden it was like something jumped up on the bed; like an animal. I knew it was not my dog because she was in her cage.

I got up and looked around...nothing. I cut the lights, out except for my nightlight. The next couple of nights it was fine. Then every other night it felt like someone, or something, was in the bed right beside me.

I sleep on my side and my husband used to be on his side next to me. It was like someone had hold of me; I couldn't move. That happened to me before also. I told David that I thought I had brought whatever was in Mrs. Beal's room up to the third floor.

Recently, I was lying in bed and I sleep with two pillows on each side. Same thing happened, like a cat or dog jumped on the bed. All of the sudden the top pillow, on the other side of where I sleep, raised up about two inches. I called my son, David, crying. He came up here to check things out but didn't see anything. He could see I was really shook up.

It happens so much that you sort of get used to it.

My physician says, "Just turn around and tell them you're not in the mood for this stuff tonight.

I was scared to death, but it continues to happen to me constantly.

Chapter 24
Black Horse Inn

Lynn Pirozzoli, Owner
8393 Meetze Road
Warrenton, Virginia 20187
Phone: 540-349-4020 Fax: 540-349-4242
Website: relax@blackhorseinn.com

History

The history of the Black Horse Inn is quite interesting and may provide us with some insight about the ghosts that frequent the Inn. Built in the 1850s, the Inn served as a hospital during the Civil War.

The Inn changed ownership many times, as the Town of Warrenton changed hands over sixty-five times from Union to Confederate and vice-versa throughout the course of the war.

In the 1920s, it was purchased by Dr. Sprague and was completely renovated with a large addition. The good doctor would bring his convalescing patients to his home from Washington, D.C. and care for them. The house was a place of healing to this point, but thereafter, the Inn was owned by several families, each occupying the house for somewhat abbreviated stays. Each time the house changed hands, it fell into greater and greater disrepair, until it was completely restored in 1992.

Some folks say that the house was cursed by a breaking of covenants each time that it changed hands. Perhaps this is why we have four ghosts that frequent the Black Horse Inn.

Ghost Stories
Told by Lynn Pirozzoli, Owner

Since the Inn served as a hospital during the Civil War, we believe that one ghost is a Civil War nurse who can be heard cheering up the soldiers. Her laughter is heard throughout the oldest section of the house and, conspicuously, only heard by our gentlemen guests.

She was first heard by one of our burley contractors that assisted us in the restoration of the Inn in 1992. Nothing fazed him and he was adamant about not believing in ghosts!

One late afternoon, at dusk of a cold winter day, he came running up the stairs to the Jeffersonian room, where I was painting. His face was pale and he was bug-eyed.

He abruptly asked if I had been downstairs laughing incessantly. I told him that I had been busy painting on the opposite side of the house for the entire afternoon. His hair stood on end and he quickly found an excuse to leave for the evening. Never again did he work beyond dusk at the Black Horse Inn.

Male guests staying at the Inn, in the oldest section, have also heard her laughter. They hear her late in the evening, usually in the comfort of their four-poster canopy bed.

Oddly enough, the laughing is that of a female voice and she is particularly inclined to laugh ONLY in men's' ears. The laughter is not threatening, but endearing and most of the gentlemen that have heard her are not unsettled. I tell them she is just trying to cheer them up, as she did in the hospital during the days when she served as a nurse at the Inn during the Civil War.

*****

Another ghost is known by the local community as "The Dancer," an apparition that can be seen at the top of the stairs, tap dancing until dawn. Some guests can hear the "tap, tap, tap" of his dancing shoes on the wooden floor.

I was first apprised of his presence by neighbors who stated that, as children, they would lay in wait for his appearance. When the neighbors ask if I have seen him of late, I respond that I meet him at the top of the stairs every night and we dance until the sun comes up! Needless to say, the local community now has a few stories about the owner!

*****

Across the hall from the dancing ghost is the Burgundy Room. It is frequented by a male ghost that enjoys sitting on the bed. The feather comforter always has a depression, where this gentleman is sitting, even shortly after the bed is freshly made up by our housekeepers. Evidently, this ghost has a sense of humor.

*****

One cold and windy winter evening, the owner crawled out the window and onto the adjoining roof to remove a dead tree limb. As she neared the edge of the roof, the screen and storm window slammed down, shutting the screen completely and leaving only a half-inch gap between the sill and the storm window. Frantically, she called for help, but to no avail. The staff could not hear her.

Tediously, the owner unraveled the screen and worked her fingers onto the base of the storm window to slide it up. Lucky for the owner that the storm window had stopped with only a half-inch gap to spare as there were no guests staying in that room that night.

*****

The final ghost only frequents the Inn at Christmas and takes great pleasure in knocking the Christmas tree over with such a vengeance that it breaks all the beautiful bulbs and ornaments. This has happened consecutively for three years.

The first time it happened was after a Christmas party specifically scheduled for naming the Inn. This was prior to the restoration, so there was nothing else in the house, save the Christmas tree in the middle of the living room. All the guests were responsible for bringing a special ornament for the tree as part of our tree-decorating extravaganza. The tree was adorned with very beautiful and special ornaments from all of our friends.

That evening, I heard a thud and breaking glass in the living room. I ran down the stairs and found the tree thrown over so forcefully that many of the ornaments had broken and were strewn over the wooden floor. I thought perhaps that this spirit must have had an exceptionally unhappy Christmas to wreak such havoc on the Christmas tree.

The second time it happened only a half-hour before a sit-down dinner for the son of a very prominent member of the community. Much to my dismay, I ran outside and secured two large cinder blocks and some bailing twine. I jury-rigged the tree in the corner, to prevent further tree-bashing during the formal dinner.

The third year, I believe that I may have exorcised the ghost. I angrily vented my displeasure at his antics at the top of my lungs for nearly a quarter of an hour, telling that ghost just what I thought of him! I now secure the tree in the corner of the room with bailing twine and hooks to prevent further mishaps!

Chapter 25
Red Garter B & B Inn

137 W Railroad Avenue
Williams, AZ 86046
(928) 635-1484 | (800) 328-1484
John Holst, owner and innkeeper

History

"I do appreciate the fact that this building has over 100 years of very traumatic things going on," Holst said, *"so anything's possible."*

The Red Garter Inn was originally built in 1897. We are about sixty miles from the Grand Canyon on old Route 66 right in the middle of Arizona on what is now Interstate 40.

The building was built as a saloon and brothel. The people who were in the area were in hopes of having a big mine nearby so they could make a lot of money. The guy who build the place figured this was a good deal for making him money too!

It worked as a brothel from 1896 until the mid 40's. A steep flight of steps known as the "Cowboy's Endurance Test" led to the girls upstairs.

The saloon was downstairs with lots of excitement, as you can imagine. People around the area still remember the big brawls that would go on in here. They had pool games, gambling in the back and the girls upstairs. They had a Chinatown where oriental railroad workers settled when the railroad was completed. There was an opium den and a little chop shack out in the back yard.

There were many occasions where the sheriff would come, thinking that he'd heard about somebody getting killed in a poker game or something like that. Maybe they had been stuffed in the old, two-story outhouse out back????

This was right in the middle of the wild and crazy old west. Route 66 came through in 1928 and this was the last town to be bypassed by the interstate system. We were the last part of the original Route 66 in 1984.

I bought the place in 1979 and by that time, it had been run down and the town was worn out. Route 66 was still here but people were worried that it was going to be a ghost town when it went away. The town dwindled down to almost nothing by the time that it became bypassed by the interstate.

This old brick building was in the middle of the downtown area. I used it to store tires and stuff until I starting rebuilding it.

I heard stories from people about one of the clients being upstairs when one of the gals killed him. They closed the whole red light district because of that particular crime. There has always been a lot of emotion that has been in both the neighborhood and the building.

I have rooms upstairs and downstairs where the saloon, was is a bakery. So people come in the bakery/gift shop to visit and see the place. Guests have their separate area upstairs so they can stay in the rooms where the girls used to live.

In the old days, the girls used to hang out the windows and wave at the cowboys as they would come down Route 66 or pass on the train that went out to Los Angeles. The girls came and went because it was a very rough place.

Route 66 goes from Chicago to Los Angeles and everything was pretty much on that "headed-west" road. "I do appreciate the fact that this building has more than 100 years of traumatic things going on" Holst continues. "So anything's possible."

Ghost Stories
Interview with John Holst
Eve

While most guests report having a good sleep, some say they felt the bed shake, heard someone going up and down the stairs or felt something touching their arms. Some people feel like there is a girl in particular, named Eve that tries to connect with people. I really don't know how she chooses them. It seems like that name has stuck with the visions or images that people have.

She generally presents herself to the guests as like a little kid would. Trying to wake up mom without scaring her sort of. Brushing on an arm or pushing on the edge of the bed to kind of wanting to get mom's attention. Very shy.

I've had ladies over the years that have mentioned that their husbands were asleep but it felt like someone was waking them up or sitting at the end of the bed. These were some of the things that we have had going over the fifteen years that I've had this bed and breakfast going.

Sometimes the men wake up in the middle of the night and see a beautiful, young Hispanic gal roaming around the room in a negligee.

A kid woke up in the middle of the night and something just pushed right through him. WHOOOOOOO and went in and closed the door in the bathroom. He got back in bed, pulled the covers over his head and stayed there. He told us about it the next morning.

Quite a few ghost hunters come through and do their investigations and some things come up the same such as cold spots or the same activity in the different instruments that they have. By and large, most of it is upstairs.

In the downstairs area they've had orbs and reflections in glass and shadow figures spotted in different parts of the area. About every couple of weeks, we'll have somebody say that something strange happened to them in the middle of the night. It's always interesting to hear what it is. Personally, I've lived in the building for a period of time and having rebuilt the building from an empty warehouse I think about plumbing, electrical, mechanical things, something loose on the roof, banging, or a big knock when I hear these noises.

Lots of creaking on the steps and pictures of a blurred, smoky image comes out on the picture that has been taken.

I'd have to say it's a mildly haunted place. We enjoy the history and having people feel it in the fabric of the building and hear a good story of two!

Chapter 26
The Inn at 835

835 South 2nd Street
Springfield, Illinois 62704
Telephone: (217) 523-4466 Fax: (217) 523-4468
E-Mail: innkeeper@innat835.com
Website: http://www.innat835.com/
Thank you to Karen Conn and Sally Hays

Located in Central Illinois, the Inn at 835 Bed & Breakfast is conveniently situated in the historic district of Springfield. For the historical enthusiast, the inn is on the old Route 66, 1926-1930.

History

The inn was designed during the Arts and Crafts Movement by one of the area's leading architects, George Helmle. The building's founder was Miss Bell Miller, a turn-of-the-century local businesswoman and florist to Springfield's high society.

Bell began her floral business in the early 1890s, when she was only in her 20s. Her trade flourished and she expanded her small floral business to a sprawl of adjacent greenhouses, which encompassed a city block. In time, Bell further expanded her business interests by building a luxurious apartment dwelling, working with George Helmle in designing her dream at 835 South Second Street.

By December of 1909, Bell had created one of Springfield's premier residences, with airy verandahs, exquisite oak detailing, and massive fireplaces to warm the heart. Situated on a corner, near the neighborhood once termed "Aristocracy Hill", the building's simple, dignified exterior design appealed to a refined sense of taste. As the years passed, an array of aristocratic tenants graced the luxury apartments.

Today, this stylish, Classical Revival structure has been fully renovated to afford you every modern convenience without detracting from the sense of gracious luxury which Bell Miller created. The inn is listed on the National Register of Historic Places and has been honored as a Springfield landmark by the City of Springfield.

The Ghosts
Told by Sally Hays, Innkeeper

I was working quietly in our offices underneath the stairs when I heard a noise. I went to investigate and some old books, which had been piled on the table, had flown off onto the floor. Nobody was around but me and there were these books...

*****

The elevator *takes you where* IT wants you to go. Push floor three and end up in the basement, for example. It's just very playful. Everyone needs a playful elevator.

*****

The Lilly Room is ice cold with a distinct smell of flowers, much like a funeral home. Nobody knows where the smell is coming from.

*****

I was working at the front desk when something ran past my peripheral vision! It was a woman in period clothing. As I looked up, she disappeared!

*****

The Orchid Room just gives me the creeps, not quite sure why.

*****

There was an old, antique clock that never worked. It was a gift to the owners and sat on the table where the books were thrown from. Suddenly, one night, it started chiming after years of not working.

*****

I have come to terms with the spirits. They are both friendly, playful, and a definite, accepted presence. But you have to get stern with them. If you are busy and they're trying to play with you, you just have to tell them, "STOP, I don't have time for this right now."

Chapter 27
Pat O'Brien's Bar

718 St. Peter Street, New Orleans, LA 70116
Main office 504-525-4823 . Direct 504-582-6908 . Fax 504-588-2864
Website: www.patobriens.com

History

Through the years, Pat O'Brien's has been and always will be an important part of New Orleans culture.

At the end of prohibition in 1933, Pat O'Brien converted his speakeasy to a legitimate drinking establishment in the 600 block of St. Peter Street called, of course, Pat O'Brien's. Business was good and the bar was always filled with neighborhood folks. There was a little upright piano in the corner for entertainment and there was always lively conversation.

A few years later, Pat realized that he had outgrown his little space. He and his friend, Charlie Cantrell, decided to become partners and buy the building at 718 St. Peter Street, the building that is now home to the world famous bar. The structures were originally built circa 1791 and became home to the first French

Theater Company in New Orleans.

In the mid 1940's Pat O'Brien's Bar propelled when the Hurricane Drink was created. At that time, there was short supply of liquor such as whiskey, bourbon, and scotch. There was, however, access to rum coming up the river. Bar owners were forced to buy large quantities of rum, fifty cases or so, in order to purchase other liquor. Through trial and error, they came up with a drink that everyone loved! Pat O'Brien paired it up with a glass shaped like a Hurricane lamp and the drink was perfected!

Under the management of George Oechsner, Jr., Pat O'Brien's quickly became the most popular bar in New Orleans. The new concept of dueling piano players in the Piano Lounge had everyone dancing in the aisles. The Main Bar was a mainstay for neighborhood friends, and the Patio a perfect place to socialize.

When he was old enough to hold a broom, Mr. Oechsner brought his son, Sonny, to help clean up. As he grew older his job duties changed, and so did his passion for Pat O'Brien's. In the late 1970's, Sonny Oechsner and his father began to buy the business with a vision of greatness.

Sonny realized the potential of the brand and pursued the concept of franchising. He also realized the need for private parties and purchased a building on Bourbon Street when opportunity arose. At this time, the company has four independently owned franchises, two restaurants in New Orleans, an online catalog, a bottling plant and endless possibilities.

Even though the corporation has branched out, the main reason for its success is the fervor of New Orleanians have for the place.

"Even though millions of people visit Pat O's every year, locals are the reason the doors stay open" says Shelly Oechsner Waguespack, Vice

President. "Locals are the heart and soul of what we are all about...passion for fun and live."

Ghost Stories
Interview given by Shelly Oechsner Waguespack

One weird thing started years ago in the office. We have been in this location since 1942. Managers would go in at night, when the place was closed, and hear strange things going on up in the attic, above the office. Nothing specific, it just sounded like footsteps walking around. They dismissed it as "Well, it's ok. It's just the ghost." This just freaked everybody out a little bit.

We purchased a building on Bourbon Street in 1989, which is now our restaurant. During the renovation of the restaurant, (we were converting it from apartments to our restaurant) several things occurred that were rather strange, mainly on the fourth floor of the building. It used to be an attic, but we turned it into an apartment/office. It is empty now.

*****

Strange things would happen while the guys were working on the building. They would close a window, leave for the day, and then the next day the window would be up. This happened several times. On the fourth floor there is always a spooky, eerie feeling so nobody likes to go up there. We had people in our sales department work up there for quite some time, but this was mainly during the day and all the odd things happened during the nighttime.

Things would be misplaced and we couldn't put a handle on it except to say "Ok, it's haunted and nobody wants to go up there. Hammers might be moved to another place or some other piece of workers' tools.

*****

A couple of years ago we have a bartender who's been working with us for quite some time. She works in the piano lounge, on the patio mostly, and on this particular day she went into the lounge to get some supplies when she heard a chair move. (This was after Katrina.) The floor is tile and the chairs are wooden, so you can hear the chair when it moves.

That completely terrified her and, of course, she went running out of the lounge and told everyone that she would not go into the lounge by herself anymore. We have heard the chair move a couple more times but it's not anything constant. We 're very close to Preservation Hall, so we chalked it up to somebody next door moving the chair. Not here, because we don't want to get spooked…convincing ourselves that it was nothing. But the bartender is absolutely convinced that the chair moved.
*****

We used to have some equipment and offices on the third and fourth floors and the kitchen is on the second floor. We have had chefs and cooks that have had to go upstairs to the fourth and third floors for a variety of things…to get more products, etc., and just from the creepiness of being up there they've refused to go up anymore. Literally, one of the cooks looked at the chef and said, "You can fire me, but I'm not going on that fourth floor!"

The first few things have sparked more and more uneasiness about it but we still have a lot of people who will not go up on the fourth floor at all. We try to laugh it all off because if we think about it a lot, it really freaks us out!
*****

When the lights go down and everybody's packing up, getting ready to go home for the night, other strange things happen. Our operations Vice President told me this story that has happened a couple of times; mostly after Katrina. The spirits had been stirred up by her but they needed to settle down again.

Charlie turned out all of the lights, including the patio lights, so it was pretty much completely dark except for the moonlight. He walked out the door and the lights flipped back on. This really frightened him. It happened a couple of times on this one night where he turned them off, started walking out the door, and they flipped back on. He checked the breakers and everything to make sure all was okay. He finally left, leaving the lights on!

Lots of spooky sounds occur on the patio when the lights go down and the excitement has left for the night.

Chapter 28
Poogan's Porch Restaurant

72 Queen Street
Charleston, SC 29401
Phone: 843/577-2337
Email: info@poogansporch.com
Website: www.poogansporch.com

History

For the last 26 years, Bobbie Ball along with her father, husband and son have owned and operated one of the most popular Southern culinary traditions in Charleston, South Carolina. The restaurant was originally a house built in 1888.

Poogan's Porch is named after a dog. A scruffy neighborhood dog, Poogan spent his time wandering from porch to porch alternately lounging around and begging for table scraps. Poogan was a good ol', down-home, Southern porch dog. He became the guardian of the newly opened restaurant and presided over the renovation process. When the doors opened for business he greeted the first customers. The restaurant's family cherished him and in his honor, the owners named the restaurant after him and his favorite resting spot— Poogan's Porch. He died of natural causes in 1979 and the building is his monument.

Since opening in 1976, Poogan's Porch has upgraded the interior of the restaurant with new elements to further enhance the traditional, Victorian-style, Charleston single house. Beautiful, Southern-inspired wall coverings, refurbished hardwood flooring and modernized china and flatware are a few of the restaurant's new features. A state-of-the-art, 1500-bottle wine cellar was built in 2005, which displays the current wine selection, which has been tripled since opening. The wine menu now boasts 250 bottles and 28 wines by the glass.

Several high profile celebrities including Paul Newman, Joanne Woodward, Lauren Hutton, Jim Carrey, Jody Foster, Joe Namath, Tennessee Williams, Barbara Streisand and James Brolin have visited and raved about Poogan's. Scenes from the 1989 movie "Champagne Charlie" starring Hugh Grant were filmed inside the popular restaurant and the walls are filled with mementos and stories reflecting the past attention.

Ghost Stories

Zoe St. Amand, a native Charlestonian who lived at the Charleston house on 72 Queen Street for a number of years prior to her death, has been spotted in various locations at various times. Sometimes at night, guest of the Mills House Hotel catch a glimpse of an old woman in a black dress waving from a second floor window of the restaurant. Police have been notified and upon investigation have found no one inside.

Employees of Poogan's have also seen glimpses of Zoe. Pots and pans have been known to crash inexplicably in the kitchen and hostesses in the past have witnessed visions of an old woman in a long black dress walking around and then disappearing.

Bobbie even had a bout with the legendary ghost-Zoe St. Amand a few years back as she tried to close the restaurant for the evening. Having difficulties setting the alarm, Bobbie was forced to contact the alarm service company. While on the phone with the technician, two of the heavy wooded bar stools crashed, a difficult thing to happen on their own. Immediately after Bobbie assessed the situation, the kitchen door slammed open…another nearly impossible occurrence as it weighs over 40 pounds. Entering inside the kitchen, Bobbie soon discovered she was alone and there was no one around to make the racket. The conclusion was Zoe was a little agitated from the alarm disruption and decided to share her disproval.

Interview with Travis McMaster, General Manager

One day Patti Byrd (my assistant manager) and I were sitting in chairs across from each other. All of the sudden she said, "Hey, why did you do that?"

"What are you talking about?"

"You threw this pen at me," Patti answered.

I told her that I didn't throw a pen at her so we looked down the hallway from the office and there was nobody else in the office.

The pen had just come across the room and hit her! Unseen hands must have wanted to get her attention.

*****

Another time one of the servers and I were setting up for a party upstairs in what used to be Zoe's bedroom. She started looking around for some shoes to change into and could only find one of them. Hum…

A few minutes later we found them in the cubby behind a cabinet. She thought I had done it. Seems like I get blamed for all of it…ha-ha.

*****

There was one time when I first started here we had had a busy night and somebody has over-rang a bottle of beer so the bartender had already opened it so we put it in ice in case anybody bought one. Of course, they didn't order that one.

As we were leaving to lock up, I poured it in a cup to take it with me. I was waiting on the foam to go down so I could drink it and I looked down and there was a heart in the foam. It looked like somebody had placed their finger in there! But, I was the only one that had handled the cup. It was in my hand the whole time I was walking around checking to make sure everything was locked up and the lights were out. I figured I might as well drink it…

*****

One time, about a year ago, a coffee pot flew across the kitchen and smashed. There were a bunch of people in the kitchen at the time and nobody saw what had caused this.

*****

I was up in the office responding to some emails and went to leave and the door was dead-bolted. It is never dead-bolted while anyone is in there and someone would have had to use a key. I was the only one in the building that had a set of keys. I unlocked it and got out real fast.

Chapter 29
Herr Tavern & Public House

900 Chambersburg Road
Gettysburg, PA. 17325
(717) 334-4332 (800) 362-9849
Website: http://www.innatherrridge.com

History

Herr Tavern was built in 1815 by Thomas Sweeney. Sweeney built his tavern here to capitalize on the route that led west. This is now US Rt. 30. It is possible that while Sweeney owned the tavern, Davey Lewis hid out here. Davey Lewis was a famous bank robber in the early 1800's. There are stories of "Lewis the Robber" using the tavern as a base of operations for counterfeiting. If this was the Davey Lewis of legend, he had to have been here when Thomas Sweeney owned the building, because Davey Lewis died in prison in Bellefonte in 1820.

Bank robbers aside, Mr. Sweeney's prosperity would not last long; Thomas Sweeney would only own the building for twelve years. In 1827 he was forced to declare bankruptcy and had to sell his tavern.

In 1828, Frederick Herr purchased the tavern that still bears his name. Frederick Herr turned the tavern into a fixture in the area; in fact, the ridge it sits on is called Herr Ridge. By all accounts, Herr ran the tavern well. He provided food, drinks and lodging for travelers as well as the locals. It seems that he also had some less than legitimate business ventures as well.

According to stories and legends, he allowed a friend to use the basement of Herr Tavern for a counterfeiting operation, too. Frederick would then launder this money through the tavern, passing it off to people heading west. There is also a story that he used the upstairs as a brothel. It seems that Mr. Herr had a much diversified portfolio.

Even though it appears that Frederick Herr used his tavern for some illegal purposes, he put it to good use as well. In the years before the Civil War, Frederick Herr allowed his tavern to be used by the Underground Railroad. No one knows how many people were helped to freedom by Mr. Herr. The Civil War removed the need rot the Underground Railroad, it also blasted through Herr Tavern.

The summer of 1863 would forever change the history of Herr Tavern. On the night of June 30th, an advanced guard of Union General John Buford's Cavalry camped on Herr Ridge. On the beginning of the next morning, July 1st, a few muskets shots were heard. These few shots soon became a torrent of fire. The Confederates of General Henry Heth pushed Buford's troops back to the outskirts of Gettysburg. What started as a minor skirmish was quickly developing into the most costly battle of the war. Herr Tavern was overrun by the Confederates, and remained behind Confederate lines for the length of the three-day battle. It is during this time that the Herr Tavern had its saddest and most traumatic use.

Herr Tavern was the nearest building to the fighting, so

naturally it was the first Confederate hospital. Several of the rooms were turned into operating theaters. It is said that amputated limbs were thrown out a window into a waiting wagon for burial.

A Civil War hospital was the closest thing to hell you could ever experience. Wounded men were everywhere. There were little or no painkillers available. The concept of sterilizing instruments was not yet known. Surgeons would wipe off their bare hands to locate the ball or piece of iron that had torn into the unfortunate patient. The smell of blood, death, and decay permeated the building. With all that energy being expended, it is no wonder that some of it still remains.

The conditions here at Herr Tavern during the battle and after were horrendous. The summer of 1863 was an unusually hot one. The first three days of July were no exception. The temperatures were in the upper 80's and the humidity was just as high. Try to imagine what it was like to be wounded and lying in the hot sun or in a sitting room waiting your turn on the surgeon's table. There is no record of how many men spent their last hours in the charnel house that the Herr Tavern had become, but it must be a truly frightening number.

Frederick Herr owned the tavern until his death in 1868. After his death the tavern was sold to the Reading family. The building was subsequently bought and sold over the years, eventually seeing use as a dairy in the early 1900's. The current owner Steve Wolf, purchased the building in 1977, and has spent the last quarter of a century turning it into the marvel that it is today. Today, the tavern shows the care and effort that Steve has put into the restoration. The tavern is a testament to Steve's dedication.

Hauntings

There are literally dozens of incidents at Herr Tavern that would indicate it is haunted.

Steve Wolf, the owner, is the first to admit that this place is haunted. Steve calls one of the ghosts "My buddy, Freddy." Steve thinks this is the ghost of Frederick Herr, although there is no way to be sure. Steve has had encounters in his tavern that have no rational explanation.

*****

One night at about 2:00 AM, Steve and a friend were closing up the tavern for the night. They were sitting at the bar ready to tally up the day's receipts when something strange happened. They both heard the door open and then the sound of footsteps coming toward them. This didn't seem unusual until they realized the door was locked. When they looked up, there was no one there.

This incident would have been strange enough, but what followed was even stranger. As they looked toward the end of the bar, both men heard a voice say "Can I order a beer?" They looked for the source of the voice, but there was definitely no one there.

While they looked on in bewilderment, the voice repeated the request "Can I order a beer?' No other words or sounds were heard, nor was anything seen. Was this a thirsty soldier looking for some relief from the hot days of battle?

*****

Steve is not the only person that works there to have experiences. Some of the staff has found forks stuck into the floor and tables amiss in the old dining room when nobody was there to do it. Glasses have scooted across tables as if they were pushed, but again, no one was there to do it. No one living, that is.

*****

One night one of the waitresses was in the kitchen and looked out towards the bar. She saw a very large man at the end of the bar. She was about to walk out and tell him that the bar was closed, but when she looked up, he had vanished. There was no way someone could have gone from the bar to the door in that brief moment of time.

*****

The kitchen is also active. The chef once heard what sounded like a whole tray of dishes crashing to the floor and breaking, but upon investigating, found nothing amiss. The same chef also heard the sound of pots and other utensils falling. Once again, nothing was out of place when checked.

*****

People have seen a woman with a baby looking out of the upstairs bedroom window. Some guests have seen a young woman with an infant in her arms walking down the stairs or heading up to the attic. People have heard a baby crying and the soft voice of a woman singing to it. Who are this woman and child? No one can say for sure, but some say it is Suzanne Herr or possibly a woman that came to wait for her husband during the Civil War.

*****

Guests have reported hearing the doors to their rooms close and lock, even though they are already closed and locked. People staying overnight have heard the doorknobs rattle as if someone is making sure they are locked. The sound of heavy booted footsteps has been heard. When the guests look out of their rooms to see who is there, the hall is always empty.

*****

Electrical appliances are not exempt from the entities that are at Herr Tavern. One night the credit card machine went crazy, it just kept rolling out paper. Lights and televisions have turned themselves on in Rooms #1 and #4.

*****

Rooms #1, #2, #3, and #4 seem to be the focus of much activity. Objects will be moved from where they were placed, doors will open and close on their own, and footsteps of an invisible intruder are heard

Chapter 30
Hotel Monteleone

214 Royal Street New Orleans, LA 70130
(504) 523-3341
Website: http://www.hotelmonteleone.com/

History

Antonio Monteleone was an industrious nobleman who was operating a very successful shoe factory in Sicily when he heard great things about America. The call of adventure motivated him to pack the tools of his trade and head for "the land of opportunity." Antonio arrived in New Orleans circa 1880 and opened a cobbler shop on Royal Street, the busy thoroughfare of commerce and banking in America's most European city.

At the time Royal Street was indeed the grand street of the "Vieux Carre", as the French Colonial's sometimes called the new town. The Hotel Monteleone has history of all sorts behind it. Being one of the premiere hotels in downtown New Orleans the Monteleone caters to the world during the famous Mardi Gras Festival.

In 1886, Mr. Monteleone bought a sixty-four room hotel on the corner of Royal and Iberville streets in New Orleans' world famous French Quarter. The setting was ripe for Antonio to spread his entrepreneurial wings when the nearby Commercial Hotel became available for purchase.

That was only the beginning of an amazing historical landmark that is one of the last great family-owned and operated hotels in the city. Since 1886, four generations of Monteleones have dedicated themselves to making their hotel what it was and still is; a sparkling jewel in the heart of the French Quarter.

There have been five major additions to the Hotel Monteleone. The first was in 1903 when 30 rooms were added. The next addition occurred in 1908, during a time of financial panic in the United States; when 300 more rooms were added. 1908 was also the year that the name of the hotel was changed from the Commercial Hotel to Hotel Monteleone.

Ghost Stories

Many people who come to Hotel Monteleone don't want to leave. Some never do...

Generations of hotel guests and staff have regularly experienced haunted events that would cause even the staunchest skeptic to take pause. This haunted hotel has a restaurant door that opens almost every evening and then closes again, even though it is locked.

*****

An elevator that stops on the wrong floor, leading a curious couple down a hallway that grows chilly and reveals the ghostly images of children playing. Hotel Monteleone is known for being one of the premier haunted hotels in North America.

*****

In March 2003, the International Society of Paranormal Research spent several days investigating Hotel Monteleone. While at the hotel, the team made contact with more than a dozen earthbound entities. Among them were several former employees, a man named William Wildemere, who died inside the hotel of natural causes, and a boy who was much older when he died, but enjoys returning to Hotel Monteleone as a 10-year-old to play hide-and-seek with another young spirit.

*****

In 1913, Antonio Monteleone passed away and was succeeded by his son Frank who added 200 more rooms in 1928, a year before another horrible crash in the U.S. economy. The Hotel Monteleone was one of America's few family-owned hotels to weather the depression, and remained unchanged until 1954. That year the fourth addition required the razing of the original building and the foundation was laid for a completely new building that would include guest facilities, ballrooms, <u>dining</u> rooms, and cocktail lounges.

*****

In 1964, under the direction of Bill Monteleone, who took over after his father passed in 1958, more floors, guestrooms, and a Sky Terrace with swimming pools and cocktail lounges were added.

*****

A successful, financial planner from California has always had an extra sense about ghosts. "I've had this eerie ability to see ghosts since I was a young child," she explains.

So it wasn't a surprise that when Mrs. P. checked into her suite on the 14th floor of Hotel

Monteleone, she had a visitor.

The historic hotel, founded in 1886 and owned by the fourth generation of the Monteleone family, has often heard ghost stories from guests, especially on the fourteenth floor (actually the thirteenth floor.)

"I was just relaxing in bed one morning when I looked up to see a young boy about three—years-old walk by the foot of my bed," she vividly recalls. "Since he had come from the sitting room, I immediately got up to see if the door was open and to check if a parent may have followed him into the room. My husband had just left for a meeting and I thought he may not have closed the door all the way."

The door was securely closed. "It didn't take me long to realize that I had seen a ghost," she continues. "He was a friendly little fellow, wearing a striped shirt. One moment he was there and the next he was gone."

The experience was so real that Mrs. P. always requests the same room when she visits the Monteleone. "I've been back twice since I first saw the child and he hasn't reappeared, but I am always thinking that maybe he will next time."
*****

The story of the young boy has been repeated many times by other guests and legend has it that he was the son of Josephine and Jacques Begere. They stayed at the Monteleone when they came to New Orleans to attend an opera in the famous French Opera House on Bourbon Street in the late 19th century.

Maurice, their young son, was left with his nanny while the couple went off to the opera. Unfortunately, an accident occurred as they were returning to the hotel. The horses bolted when they heard a loud noise and Jacques was thrown from the buggy, killing him instantly. They say that Josephine died within a year of a broken heart.

The speculation is that the ghost of young Maurice sometimes roams the halls searching for his parents. His presence is especially felt on the fourteenth floor near the room where his parents were staying.

CPSIA information can be obtained at www.ICGtesting.com
231331LV00003B/158/P